Praise for the 2007

"One of the greatest accounts of Sixties rock 'n' roll"

THE INDEPENDENT

"Spence, collaborator on Stoned, delivers the lowdown on the controversial and prestigious British Record label"

WATERSTONES

"The sound of the Sixties"

CLASH

"Spence used inside knowledge to produce this definitive book about the maverick independent label"

THE BEAT

"Sheer brilliance flashes from many of the interviewees"

DAVE THOMPSON

"A story worth reading"

SPIN

"Perhaps the most fascinating part of this book is the last chapter where Spence relates some of his experiences of working with ALO - the two of them together in Oldham's sanctuary of Bogota, Colombia[1]."

SHINDIG

---

1. This is now the Author's Note - p.vii

IMMEDIATE

"Fuck Them All"

The Rise and Fall of the UK's First
Independent Record Label

By Simon Spence

BB

backstage books

www.backstage-books.com

First published 2007

This edition published 2023

© Backstage Books 2023

BACKSTAGE BOOKS

10 Cambridge Rd, Hale, Cheshire WA15 9SZ

ISBN: 978-1-7394779-0-5

Printed in Great Britain

Contents

Andrew Loog Oldham

A REFERENCE

S imon first came into my life as a reporter for the UK based *Face* magazine when he visited me at my home in Bogota, Colombia, to interview me for various articles on British managers of rock 'n' roll in the sixties and the groups I managed at that time.

As a result of this I engaged him in 1996 to be the investigative reporter, researcher and "interviewer of voices" for my biographies *Stoned* and *2Stoned*.

I found his research detailed and professional, his investigative abilities inspired, all of which made his interviews first-rate and, with his ability to track and authenticate the time-line, we worked on a professional level resulting in works that have been well-received and applauded as more than mere autobiography but historical reference points of the era.

Simon was aware of this agenda and did a remarkable job in assisting me in bringing my life and times to the table.

Acknowledgements

As much as I enjoy the music of Immediate, the real stars of the label will always be Andrew Loog Oldham and Tony Calder. Charly and Universal may hold the worldwide copyright to the back catalogue but the true spirit and story of Immediate Records will always belong to these two peerless music industry pioneers.

Salut to Kevin Pocklington (it's been a long time coming but here it is) and eternal gratitude to Esther and Max for making Colombia a home away from home. Special thanks to Ashley Shaw, editor of this book, for his guidance and for writing all the footnotes and to Anthony Donnelly, publisher and polymath - we're all ten foot tall in your company.

Author's Note

AN EXPLANATION

In *NME*'s 'Loudmouth' section, which was a box-out on the gossip/joke page rounding up a few of the week's most notable *bon mots*, the legendary former Rolling Stones manager and founder of Immediate Records, Andrew Loog Oldham, was quoted thus: "Simon reminds me of the son I never wanted."

That was in 1991. Looking back, not just at this book, first published in 2008 (of which more later) but over a music journalism career that now spans 34 years, I'll allow myself to add my own reciprocal quote: "Andrew became the father I never wanted".

There is little of Oldham's Immediate adventure in his two volumes of autobiography: *Stoned* and *2Stoned*. Oldham and I spent almost a decade working together on his memoirs, at first intermittently and then full-time between 1996 and 1999. We talked about the label in depth; I'd heavily researched it and interviewed scores of people on the subject.

So, having seen that most of this research had been consigned to the cutting room floor I patched together a book about the label that was published by Black Dog in 2008. They'd done a few similar graphic-led 'coffee table' style books on labels such as Rough Trade and Warp. My then-editor, can you believe it, was the now celebrated and *Vogue*-affiliated and sometimes *Times* columnist, Raven Smith. He was an intern working for kudos, fucking useless but he saw it through, so God bless. It was something of a blessing for me when the error-strewn book developed cover lamination problems and all remaining copies were pulped.

I did a talk about the book at Waterstones' Gower Street branch in London and Tony Calder turned up to lend support. The reviews were good, a page lead in *Mojo* with a pic of the book cover and a larger pic of the Small Faces (the book received four stars and described as 'essential and exhilarating').

Black Dog sent me more reviews but I didn't really know the mags well [websites now I guess]: *Clash*, *Goldmine* (reviewed by Dave Thomson who went on to work with ALO after me) and *Shindig*. One review started: "In the mid-60s ALO was the king of hip" and described me as "a former *NME/Face* writer who has had quite a history working alongside ALO".

The review continued: "Initially hoping to write ALO's biography, Spence eventually did much of the legwork on Oldham's autobiography *Stoned* and *2Stoned*. Perhaps the most fascinating part of the book is the last chapter, where Spence relates some of his experiences working with ALO in this process – the two of them together in Oldham's private sanctuary of Bogota, Colombia, Oldham's behaviour wildly unpredictable."

In 1990 I'd first read about Oldham in *Starmakers and Svengalis*, a book given me by *NME* reviews editor, Stuart Bailie. It was a turnaround for Bailie who had previously had to be pulled away from physically attacking me in the *NME* office after I had bad-mouthed Van Morrison in either print or in person.

The chapter in *Starmakers and Svengalis* that focused on Oldham was addictive stuff. The architect of The Rolling Stones' golden years — a visionary teenage pop genius in dark glasses, make-up and sharp suits, his story full of drugs, guns, gangsters, cash, chaos and controversy. The book said that, at the end of the sixties, when he was just

26, Oldham had simply disappeared. "Burnt out like a light bulb," Keith Richards quipped.

Oldham was mentioned here and there in scores of Stones books but his huge impact on the group had never been fully documented. What sent me wild was Nik Cohn — in his 1969 seminally-regarded speed-read breakdown of the era's pop giants, *Awopbopaloobop Alopbamboom* he called Oldham "without doubt, the most flash personality that British pop has ever had, the most anarchic and obsessive and imaginative hustler of all".

I know Oldham prefers what George Melly wrote about him in the 1970 book *Revolt In Style*, that he was "as pretty and cunning as a stoat" but both Melly and Cohn's main emphasis in their descriptions was Oldham's overt manipulation of the Stones, particularly Mick Jagger.

I started digging around. Gered Mankowitz — the photographer famed for capturing the Stones in their mid-sixties prime — assured me Oldham was still alive although, dispiritingly, living far away in Colombia.

He gave me the number of Allen Klein's office in New York, the best way he knew of getting a message to Oldham, then asked that I didn't mention his assistance if I did manage to contact the Loog saying that he didn't need the obscene phone calls to start up again.

There was gossip and hearsay: essentially, that he was unhinged after thirty years of living in Colombia, lost in a drugs and booze hinterland; his mind beset by demons, he lived life on a knife edge and was quick to violence.

Allen Klein had succeeded Oldham as Stones' manager and had a reputation as a real Mafia heavy. I had the cheek to promise him I was going to ring his office every day until I got a response from Oldham. It worked. About a week later the telephone rang. It was true. Oldham was nuts. I couldn't follow much of what he was saying but what he did say, in this low menacing gnash, seemed to have undercurrents of deep portent. I was blown away. Suddenly the phone went dead. Through the crackling, unreliable lines to Colombia — a country suffering power surges and blackouts — did I actually hear him say, "If you get over here there might be a book in it for you".

I was a happy 21 when the editor of *The Face*, Sheryl Garrett, gave me the opportunity to find out, paying cash up front for a piece about the trip to Colombia that I had pitched as a journey to a heart of musical darkness to uncover my rock 'n' roll Colonel Kurtz.

At that time Colombia was quite intense. Infamous drug lord Pablo Escobar was engaged in an all-out war with the authorities and bombs, kidnaps and shootings were commonplace in the capital city, Bogotá, where Oldham lived. As far as I had been able to ascertain I was his first press visitor from the UK.

Oldham wasn't at the airport to meet me and my *NME* photographer pal Martyn Goodacre as agreed and when I called ALO grumbled that we had arrived a day early. Forty minutes later we were in a lift riding to the top of a classy uptown residential tower, to Oldham's triplex apartment where he sat in a big room on the second floor, half hidden in the shadows, mumbling.

We stayed seven days. Oldham snorted a helluva lot of cocaine and drank a tremendous amount of grappa. He was razor thin, wild, wired, almost reptilian in appearance and his eyes bulged as he regurgitated unfathomable tales that went on until daybreak and made my head ache. He didn't seem to need sleep and ate off a tray in front of a giant screen television invariably playing gangster movies featuring Christopher Walken whose mannerisms and looks he sometimes aped while we were together. He rarely ventured further than the local drug store for more cigarettes but we did take a memorable trip around the city's charming barrios.

He shared some cocaine but mostly slipped off to the bathroom to consume it. Between the booze and coke, we smoked high-grade marijuana. He didn't smoke many joints normally on account of his hands being too shaky to get it together.

Oldham showed us his collection of knives, sunglasses and jewellery and spoke about a gun. He changed his outfits quite outrageously throughout the day. He was impossible to fathom. He told me he had struck a book deal in the US sometime in the eighties for half a million dollars but had to cancel it when he pushed the writer into a nervous breakdown.

By the end of the week Martyn and I were wrecks and now we were forced to make a frantic escape from Bogotá. The return journey was full of chaos and confusion; there were elections going on and the streets of Bogotá were full of angry crowds. I remember someone gobbing in my face. There was more terror at the airport with people screaming and demands for money. I think they were after the airport tax but Martyn and myself were so high by then, our paranoia reaching such dizzy heights, that we thought we may be trapped forever in this madness. Once on board the plane Martyn thought he saw God and his face froze in terrifying fear for more than ten minutes and I was sure he'd had a heart attack.

Landing for our connection in Paris I fumbled my passport handing it over to be checked and told the guard to "Pick it up yourself". We were detained, stripped and urine tests showed our cocaine levels to be riding nice and high.

When I got down to piecing the week together I turned to my notes - a bundle of barely decipherable hand-written reminiscences of Oldham's early childhood on fast fading fax paper and an overwhelming amount of rambling interview tapes that I transcribed. When it came to do *The Face* article, I struggled to pull one usable short quote from the entire lot.

Six months later Oldham came to London and the

possibility of a book seemed more real now, but he stated it would only profile his life up until he was 19 — the year he became manager of the Stones. He holed himself up in an expensive suite in the Royal Lanesborough hotel on Hyde Park Corner for a fortnight where we would start sessions well after midnight which would run through the night with Oldham sat in dark glasses; drink in hand, openly snorting coke off the table. A daylight meeting — buying books for research in Soho — was a nervy, sweaty and awkward experience for both of us, but by evening it was forgotten and in the cool of his hotel room the information piled up; an overwhelming jumble of names and events, with the sequences of his formative experiences forever shifting.

Throughout his stay there were inexplicable appearances from heavy looking Russians in the night, heated exchanges, then straight back in to a ridiculous story about a camel hair overcoat he once wore to a French new wave film showing at the Hampstead Everyman in 1960 — or was it the fake fur zebra-print drape stolen from a strip club in Nice the same year?

I was lapping it up. As word got round about the book, he leaked *NME* the quote about me.

He was born in Paddington, London in January 1944, shortly after his father, Andrew Loog, a US fighter pilot of Dutch heritage, was shot down and killed over Belgium. Andrew's mother, Celia, had emigrated as a kid with her mother from Australia to London. She spent her 20s dragging "Andy" between various north-west London rented rooms and apartments, a strong single mother.

One of Oldham's earliest memories was of finding a flatmate of Celia's dead, with her head in the oven. Before he was in double figures his mother took a lover, millionaire Jewish businessman Alec Morris, who'd made his fortune in furniture.

As a father figure Alec was flash. He drove a Rolls Royce, dressed well and regularly took Oldham to the famous Ivy restaurant. Celia, who was half-Jewish herself — her father having fled to Australia from Poland — eventually settled in a ground floor apartment in Hampstead and that stylish, artistic suburb became Oldham's manor. There were no relations at hand and, despite the boyfriend, the family wasn't rich. Celia worked as a part-time Comptometer (the predecessor of the modern computer) operator and Oldham learned to be independent. In his first year at Marylebone state school, aged 11, he was expelled for extortion.

When he became famous much was made of the "public-school educated" Oldham. A burst of private tuition helped him though the 11-plus and he was hurried off to Wellingborough, a 400-year-old public school near Northampton that was full of farmers' children. He stuck out, flouncing up from London in tailor-made Teddy Boy drape suits, inventing a long-running dental problem that allowed him to escape back to the city whenever he chose.

Oldham worked hard at being stylish and was full of self-assurance, impressing Wellingborough school pals by appearing in the audience of the legendary television pop show *Oh Boy!* He recalled holidays spent pounding the streets of London, knocking on the doors of show-business impresarios, directors, actors and music companies. Age 12 his mother took him to see the West End stage production of *Expresso Bongo*, a black comedy about the music business starring Soho Johnny Jackson and teen rock 'n' roller Bongo Herbert. It was made into a film in 1959 starring Laurence Harvey as sharp-elbowed Tin Pan Alley manager Johnny and Cliff Richard as Bongo. The stage production and film made a lasting impression, as did Elvis, James Dean, Marlon Brando, Jimmy Greaves and Jet Harris. Leaving school at 16 with one O-level and no chance of higher education, his final school report read, "Andrew may do well, but not here"[1].

Too sharply dressed for Hampstead's burgeoning 1960-61 beatnik coffee bar scene, Oldham became a sort of proto-Mod, perfecting the pose with his first real ally, the infamous Peter Meaden[2], aka 'The Face', who later with Phil 'The Greek' as bodyguard, orchestrated the early career of The Who. The two hung out at trendy clothes shops — John Michael's and Austin's — and hip clubs such as The Scene. They shopped, popped pills, and partied until they dropped. They tried their hand at PR (for John Michael) and gig promotion and started to get a bit of a reputation as a likely pair.

Oldham got a write-up and picture of himself in the first ever British men's fashion page, which appeared in the *Evening Standard*, touting grey flannel shirts as the next big thing. His first major piece of luck came at 17 when he landed a job running errands for Mary Quant at her King's Road Bazaar boutique. "The carpets were thick and the teacups thin," he quipped and he had a front row seat as Quant revolutionised women's fashion. He soon found himself in the papers again, this time in a lead feature in the *Daily Mail*, full of himself for conning Burton's into making

---

1. Laurence Harvey, born Zvi Mosheh Skikne, (1928–1973) was a Lithuanian born actor and film director best known for his clipped, refined accent and cool, debonair screen persona. His performance in *Room at the Top* (1959) brought him an Academy Award nomination. That success was followed by the roles of William Barret Travis in *The Alamo* and Weston Liggett in *Butterfield 8*, both films released in the autumn of 1960. He also appeared as the brainwashed Sergeant Raymond Shaw in The *Manchurian Candidate* (1962). He made his directorial debut with *The Ceremony* (1963), and continued acting into the 1970s until his premature death in 1973 of cancer.
2. Peter Alexander Edwin Meaden (1941–1978) was an English publicist for various musicians and the first manager of The Who. He was a prominent figure in the English Mod subculture of the early 1960s. He is sometimes referred to as the "Mod Father" or "Mod God" and his influence left an indelible mark on the Mod subculture.

him a 50-guinea Madras suit on the back of their £2 tailor-
made offer.

During the six months he worked for Quant he also
picked up night jobs at Ronnie Scott's Jazz Club and at
the notorious all-night Soho R&B club, The Flamingo.
Then he quit London suddenly, having something of a
breakdown, tripping off to the South of France, hustling the
show business types known to frequent exclusive enclaves
such as Juan Les Pins. There he met theatre and song king
Lionel Bart[3] for the first time and got work at the open-
air Antibes Jazz festival where Ray Charles performed.
Oldham also got involved in a kidnapping, a stunt involving
a willing London débutante from a well-to-do family, and
sold the story back to the UK papers for cash and bumped
into Picasso smoking a joint as the artist admired his own
work in a gallery window.

Back in London for 1962 he charmed himself into a
position as a music PR, earning a stint with big Top 10
UK solo star Mark Wynter[4]. He also handled visiting US
acts such as Little Richard, Sam Cooke, Phil Spector and
Bob Dylan, and became well known to London's most-
influential music journalists, DJs, managers, agents and
record company staff.

A fortuitous meeting with Brian Epstein at the first
television appearance by The Beatles [Mark Wynter was
also on the show, called *Thank Your Lucky Stars*] led to Oldham
landing the PR job for the Mop Tops, and took great pride
in getting them in *Vogue* in early 1963. He had the ability
to make the acts "feel like a million dollars" remembered
Kenny Lynch, another of his early UK PR clients. Lynch

---

3. Lionel Bart (1930 – 1999) was a British writer and composer of pop
music and musicals. He wrote Tommy Steele's *Rock with the Caveman*
and was the sole creator of the musical *Oliver!* (1960).

4. Born Terence Sidney Lewis (1943-) Wynter had four Top 20 singles
in the 1960s, including 'Venus in Blue Jeans' and 'Go Away Little
Girl'.

added, with a smile: "He had more front than Selfridges".

That took us up to his discovery of The Rolling Stones, but Oldham was still holding out on sharing those golden years with me. Despite this several publishers showed interest in our material. We kept in contact until Oldham relaunched Immediate Records with his original partner in the label, Tony Calder, in 1993. The band[5] I fronted at the time had just been dropped by Pete Waterman's PWL — the promise of Kylie producing our debut album and our own label, PWL Rock, having failed to materialise. We took the opportunity to jump on board Immediate III, making a video – payment for which was delivered in £50 notes in a brown paper envelope.

Oldham returned to London to promote the venture, greeting me with a Nazi salute and immediately snorting half the six grams of coke he asked me to bring him. Journalists queued up to talk to him in his room at the Draycott Hotel in Chelsea, where a large framed still of Al Pacino in *The Godfather 3* had pride of place. Martyn's Colombia shots of him ended up on the cover of the *Independent Magazine*.

He was a great read: "Legendary... brilliant... eccentric gangster" swigging from his bottle of grappa, "veering drunkenly between warm geniality and raging indignation". A songwriter passing through made a comment about the physical attributes of his Colombian actress wife, Esther, to which Oldham reacted by punching the man's groin, telling an astounded onlooking journalist: "He's lucky he didn't get killed" as the man writhed on the floor.

Stones biographer David Dalton — then finishing the Marianne Faithfull biography — was humiliated by Oldham; the contents of his bag, full of Christmas

---

5. The original line-up of Fabulous was: your author (vocals), Martyn Goodacre (guitar), Russell Underwood (guitar), Kieron "Ronnie Fabulous" Flynn (bass) and Robert "Hodge" Hodges (drums).

gifts, unceremoniously dumped on the floor in front of a assortment of Oldham's business associates and hangers-on.

Throughout his stay Oldham was on a short fuse — interpreting teasing remarks as slurs and at least once hurling a plate of food at the wall. One journalist noted him "rolling around on the carpet, feet swinging in the air, bellowing, 'We all live in a yellow submarine', at the top of his voice".

Another evening, around midnight, I was summoned to bring what I had of the book so far. The room was crowded with Annie and the Scream wrecking crew and the detritus of a wild drugs and booze party. Oldham was drunk and just wanted to tell me I was finished. What he said during a ten-minute dressing down was difficult to follow but could be summed up as 'don't kid a kidder' or 'never hustle a hustler'. He escorted me out of the room with his arm round my shoulder and in that lonely hotel corridor he half-apologised for his behaviour, with a you-know-me by now shrug.

After Immediate III collapsed without a release, two years went by without news on the book. I had expected someone else to jump on Oldham's story after that kind of publicity but nothing seemed to materialise. One night I called him in Colombia and founding him singing from a different hymn sheet. He said he'd had a radical life-style change and to meet him in Buenos Aires where he would tell me all about it.

I hustled *Arena* magazine for the air ticket and he welcomed me to his hotel suite with a non-alcoholic beer. It was still early days on his road to recovery from the booze and drugs addiction that had almost killed him. I watched befuddled as he prepared his daily intake of nutritional pills from scores of prescription bottles on his dressing table while he told me that his lifestyle change was something to do with Scientology.

In Buenos Aires he was producing his fifth album with Argentina's biggest rock 'n' roll act, The Ratones Paranoicos, for Sony South America. We'd meet in the late morning and he would buy lunch. He would then get picked up and be driven to the outskirts of the city to produce the album and retire early for a decent night's rest. I went to the studio with him once or twice; it was set in beautiful countryside and had an outdoor pool. The band, Argentina's answer to U2, were open, friendly and polite to me, despite the fact they had won big prizes on prime-time television award shows and played sold out stadium gigs.

When I wasn't with Oldham I busied myself booking appointments to meet all the major record companies, getting embroiled in some sort of oil shortage situation affecting vinyl at Polydor and chased out of Sony (who did kindly stick me a few quid for spends). There were many blasts downtown hanging out at the infamous TCT magazine shop, uptown with transvestite club runners or in photocopying shops like department stores, making up tens of one-off t-shirts.

And now, finally, I had what he told me one morning was his "blessing" to do his biography — this time I'd get everything, no holds barred. Back home I stalled on delivering the *Arena* piece (although I had taped hours and hours of interview with Oldham) I got an agent, an understudy of the man who would go on to handle the *Harry Potter* franchise. A year of paper research later (thanks darlin') and I had roughly outlined Oldham's sixties heyday to add to our exhaustive pre-Stones beginnings.

In late '96 Oldham was happy to welcome me back to Bogotá for a month. He would help me put the book together, without credit, and wanted to okay the final manuscript. He was still clean — his home life now a picture of calm. We camped in his teenage son's room to work on the only computer in the house, and then after a smooth couple of weeks he jetted off to the US for the induction of Phil Spector in to the Rock 'N' Roll Hall Of Fame. His wife, Esther, arranged a holiday for my girlfriend and I, taking in the country's contrasting *Miami Vice*-esque areas and beautifully untouched coastlines.

There followed a glorious year or more of extensive interviews with Oldham's contemporaries. He had supplied me with some phone numbers and from there the participants in the book grew until the list reached over 300 — from childhood friends through to some of the most powerful and influential people the music business has ever known.

In 1998 I travelled back to Bogotá for what was supposed to be a final two weeks getting our house in order. This stay stretched to over three months, taking in a Christmas and New Year. He was rigorous and we worked every day from early in the morning until late afternoon and finally had about 600,000 words down.

We went for Christmas dinner in a remote hotel out in the jungle owned by an English pal of his, driving three hours out of Bogotá into real guerrilla territory. I heard gunshots, screams and rustlings throughout the night. Oldham didn't seem too worried and enjoyed driving the mountainous curves in his Lexus at dizzying speeds.

I was flat broke for most of the stay in Bogotá but there were kids with carrier bags full of cheap grass on the streets and I found a Galaxian in a games arcade full of 1980s retro machines to while away the odd hour.

One evening I blacked-out while trying to pay in a cheap chicken joint and came around on the floor in front of the counter in a puddle of blood, piss and loose change. I returned to work the next morning with a black eye and scabby eyebrow. Oldham didn't mind, he was a real laugh, never taking himself seriously, but he could be a cunt. He joked at the dinner table, after he dropped a scrap of food on the floor, who would be first to it: his beloved dog Ruby or me?

Nevertheless the publishers were happy when the book was delivered but Oldham wasn't satisfied and I became worried when, on the advice of Allen Klein, he took the work to New York where it would be edited afresh.

I saw that edit when he came to London to deliver it to the publisher. Crucially, it was now all in the first person — but that's just the way it was. Oldham had approximately halved the work and the first volume, *Stoned*, followed his life until just after he met the Stones — keeping his golden era with them for a second book, *2Stoned*.

I was working in Hong Kong when *Stoned* eventually came out in 2000. I wasn't on the front cover but on page one credited with "research and interviews". In 2002, *2Stoned* came out and I received the same page one credits. In the acknowledgments Oldham wrote: "Simon Spence conducted the interviews and gathered the research upon which both *Stoned* and *2Stoned* were founded. Simon made my life and times his agenda whilst I was losing the first and pissing on the second and for that I say thank you."

Oldham's friend, famed photographer Mick Rock[6], told me I had got lucky when I bemoaned my lot to him over being dumped as 'writer'. He said if I had met Oldham, as he had in his wiry NY coke and smack splattered 1970s, I would have got really fucked over.

They say you should never meet your heroes. I was 21 when I first met Oldham. In the subsequent 32 years of knowing him; in his home, on manoeuvres, out of his head, straight, on business, in restaurants, out window shopping, lounging in hotel rooms, in a passenger seat or over the rack, he has never let me down or failed to live up to that billing. I

6. Born Michael Edward Chester Smith (1948 – 2021), Rock is often referred to as "The Man Who Shot the Seventies", being responsible for most of the memorable photos of Ziggy Stardust in his capacity as David Bowie's official photographer.

guess you just gotta choose your heroes more carefully.

Here I would like to add a special word about Tony Calder who died in 2018. This wonderful, sharp, shrewd and entertaining operator is still largely unrecognised by the modern-day cold custard music industry but have no doubt, he is one of the great UK record men. I spent the final years of his life getting to know him better, working on a film based on the story of Immediate Records.

Quite simply, Immediate wouldn't have happened without him. In early 1965 Calder was 22 and running the PR company Image, while also managing Marianne Faithfull who Oldham had launched to stardom in 1964 with the single 'As Tears Go By'.

He had met Oldham in 1963 and had been working behind the scenes on the Stones unheralded, having a particular hand in promoting 'Little Red Rooster', the Stones late '64 UK No 1, while Oldham grabbed the headlines. He'd come to London from his hometown of Southampton at 18 as a Decca Sales and Marketing trainee. He quit soon after meeting Oldham, worked as a DJ on Jimmy Savile's hugely popular 'Off The Record' Mecca Dance Hall tours and also ran his own Mod night at the Ilford Mecca, while dabbling in public relations and management, including for a very young pre-Small Faces Steve Marriott.

Image was Oldham and Calder's joint business. It was pop's first independent PR company, handling accounts for Brian Epstein's Liverpool stable and the Manchester-based Kennedy Street Enterprises' roster that featured Herman's Hermits, Freddie and the Dreamers, The Hollies, Dave Berry and Wayne Fontana and the Mindbenders, while also looking after the Stones, Gene Pitney, Georgie Fame, Kenny Lynch, Phil Spector, The Beach Boys and US TV star Dick Clark of *American Bandstand* fame.

In *Stoned* Andy Wickham, who left EMI's press office to

assist at Image and later moved to Immediate, remembered Calder as "like a dog-track bookie" who "seemed to think only in terms of deals and reeked of danger".

Tony Hall, who led Decca's surprisingly hip promotions department (largely because it was in a separate West End building to their Embankment HQ), told me: "I remember Calder rubbing his hands together, saying 'Who can we screw up now, who can we cut up'. Oldham changed when Calder came on to the scene. There was an extra element. Together they used to try and come up with every conceivable scam."

Calder told me bluntly: "Our attitude towards the business in the UK was 'fuck them all', they were all old men."

They adopted a classic good cop/bad cop routine, although Calder was as soft-hearted as Oldham at his core. They looked the part too: Oldham was tall, slim and fair-haired, Calder, broader, dark and shorter with thick-rimmed glasses. Oldham's role was the creative showman while Calder played the soberly attired suit in the background.

Since Oldham had signed the Stones to Decca he had recorded a series of acts for the label, the most successful of which were Marianne Faithfull, Vashti[7] and The Poets. The senior figures at Decca HQ, including boss Sir Edward Lewis, however, made no secret of their dislike for him, describing him as "mad as a hatter".

Calder was with him all the way, even when Oldham employed the unhinged chauffeur Reg King, who had previously worked for Brian Epstein and Lionel Bart, and tore up London streets in an open-top powder blue

---

7. Vashti Bunyan, born Jennifer Vashti Bunyan was introduced to ALO by an agent and in June 1965 released her first single, 'Some Things Just Stick in Your Mind'. Foresaking her music career after a brief appearance in *Tonite Let's All Make Love in London*, she travelled to the Herbides with her then-boyfriend to join a commune planned by Donovan.

Chevrolet Impala. "At a time," Keith Richards wryly noted, "when you didn't see that many powder blue Chevys on the street." There were endless rumours about King, Calder and Oldham: smashing passing car windows and punching pedestrians while driving the wrong way up the pavements of one-way streets. King, an expert joint roller, kept a truncheon in the car and Keith Richards gave him the sobriquet 'The Butcher'.

With The Butcher in tow rumours abounded of the trio slamming down windowsills on journalist's fingers, kicking music promoters to a pulp in the Scotch of St James nightclub[8] and assaulting Bill Cotton[9], head of BBC light entertainment. The fracas with Cotton actually served to enhance the Stones' surly performance on fading BBC pop show *Juke Box Jury*[10] that left middle-England choking; a performance about which Oldham said: "If they'd have gone down well it would have set our work back four or five months."

Oldham went public with damning assessments of British music industry. In a 1964 centre spread splash in *The Sun* he attacked the "nine-to-five mentality" at the four dominant major labels of the time: EMI, Decca, Pye and Philips, describing their offices as "funeral parlours". He criticised the ageing staffers who, after a day of putting up with "pop", go home to listen to Mantovani[11], "what they

---

8. The Scotch of St. James was where a then-unknown Jimi Hendrix first performed on the night of his arrival in England on 24 September 1966, joining the house band for an impromptu session on stage.

9. Sir William Frederick Cotton CBE (1928–2008) was a BBC producer and executive appointed Head of Light Entertainment (1970-77) and Controller of BBC1 (1977-81).

10. The music panel show hosted by David Jacobs which ran between 1959 and 1967. Of the Stones appearance on 4 July 1964 Keith Richards later wrote "We didn't give a shit.... We just trashed every record they played."

11. Annunzio Paolo Mantovani (1905 – 1980) was an Anglo-Italian

consider good music".

Oldham was already conceiving something akin to
Immediate back then. In a *Daily Mirror* spread — under
the headline, "Nut or Genius?" — Oldham claimed his
future plans included: "Buying a house in North London,
a sort of House of Talent. I will have writers there and
music arrangers. It will house only artists and equipment
to produce my records, a complete unit of talent. Writers
will have their own rooms with electric pianos. This may
sound expensive but they will be my writers, my artists, my
publishing company, and therefore my productions."

In May 1965, just prior to launching Immediate, Oldham
began ramping up his attacks on the music establishment
from a new platform as 'Britain's Most Controversial' music
columnist in the 300,000 circulation *Disc and Music Echo*
weekly magazine (an arrangement that ran for a lively six
months often under the 'Oldham Hits Out!' headline).

He wrote that the "stalwarts in the business have no
idea what is going on". It seems quaint now but at the time,
when the chairman of EMI Records Sir Joseph Lockwood[12]
had joined Sir Edward Lewis[13] and the BBC to petition the
Government to outlaw pirate radio[14] stations, Caroline and

---

light-orchestra conductor and composer described as "Britain's most
successful album act before The Beatles".

12. Sir Joseph Flawith Lockwood (1904–1991). In early 1954, he was
approached by Sir Edward de Stein to join the board of EMI who were
losing half a million pounds per year and on the verge of bankruptcy.
Lockwood oversaw substantial growth in EMI's involvement in
the record industry, buying and developing the American Capitol
company in the late 1950s, and appointing George Martin to take
charge of the Parlophone label.

13. Sir Edward Roberts Lewis (1900 – 1980) headed the Decca group
for five decades from 1929, building the company up from nothing to
one of the major record labels in the world.

14. Pirate radio became widespread in the early 1960s when pop
music stations such as Radio Caroline and Radio London started to
broadcast on medium wave to the UK from offshore ships or disused

London, Oldham was vocal in print in his backing of the new young pirate stations, a "breath of fresh air".

By this point Oldham was rich, celebrated, young and famous: his name blared out from the cover of Stones records and profiles described him as "the sixth Stone". It was well-known he'd been the one to force Jagger and Richards into writing their own material.

His major inspiration for starting Immediate came from the US. He was a regular visitor — with and without the Stones — and had forged valuable business contacts, soaking up the influence of producers such as Phil Spector and Bob Crewe[15], bathing in the 15 or so independent radio stations in New York alone. He saw how independent record labels such as Chess, Philles, Roulette, Atlantic and Motown, owned a massive slice of the US business, alongside the major labels, CBS, RCA and Capitol.

Calder and Oldham both recall Immediate actually coming to life sometime in July 1965 in the red leather back seats of a newly acquired car — an ostentatious white Lincoln Continental. The two were on the way to a television recording of *Ready Steady Go!*[16] when they told Reg

---

sea forts. At the time, these stations were not illegal because they were broadcasting from international waters. The stations were set up by entrepreneurs and music enthusiasts to meet the growing demand for pop and rock music, which was not catered for by BBC Radio. By 1967 ten pirate radio stations were broadcasting to an estimated daily audience of 10-15 million. In response to the popularity of pirate radio, BBC radio restructured in 1967 establishing BBC Radio 1, 2, 3 and 4. A number of DJs of the newly formed Radio 1 came from pirate stations. The UK Government closed the international waters loophole via the Marine Broadcasting Offences Act of 1967, although Radio Caroline would continue to broadcast in various forms right up to 1990.

15. Robert Stanley Crewe (1930–2014) was an American manager and record producer best known for producing, and co-writing a string of Top 10 singles for The Four Seasons.

16. *Ready Steady Go!* was a British rock/pop music television

to pull over at a phone box.

Calder called the Head of Philips, Leslie Gould.

Oldham told me: "The UK industry was just plodding along and I was fed up with being mocked as crazy. Tony and I agreed and decided that controlling the making of music was one thing, now we wanted to control the destiny of the music: the meeting of image, aura, art and commerce."

When dealing with the cash figures in this book, it's easiest for me to just give you 1960s amounts. £1 then is worth about £23 today (2023).

-----

programme broadcast every Friday evening from 9 August 1963 until 23 December 1966. The show went out early on Friday evenings and was famous for the line "The weekend starts here!".

Hang On Sloopy

An extract from Oldham's *Disc and Music Echo* column, August 1965: "On many occasions I have run down the large record companies over issues such as pirate stations, their promotion and their tastes. And many readers have written in and said that if I was so disturbed by the state of the existing record companies why didn't I do something about it. I have!

"On the twentieth of this month the first of three records released by my own record company, Immediate Records, is to be launched. I would like to tell you a little about the activities and the functions of Immediate Records, and about some of the things we are trying to do.

"Immediate Records will operate in the same way as any good small independent in America, with the accent on promotion and product not board meetings. We will try to set a standard of only quality records and it is our intention to release from the initial week no more than two records a week. My partner in this venture is Mr Tony Calder who, apart from being the Vice President of the Former Managers of Marianne Faithfull, (I am the President), has the most successful publicity and promotions operation going, which has handled artists like Herman's Hermits, The Beach Boys, Wayne Fontana and the Mindbenders and Marianne Faithfull. Tony will be applying his genius for promotion, his years of experience in the retail and distribution side of Decca and his years as consultant to one of the largest chain of ballrooms, in our new venture. We are very, very excited by our first three records and I would like to point out that this record company is no hobby horse for my own products.

"Immediate Records represents a growth in my activities and whereas up to now, I have just admired producer's products, I now have the opportunity, through Immediate Records, to be their associate. We will be bringing in new producers while our main hope lies with the top session guitarist turned producer, Jimmy Page, and my two friends, Mick Jagger and Keith Richard. All these three, I believe, will develop and become fine hit-making producers.

"Our first record is from the new independent company in America headed by that gigantic hit-maker and songwriter Bert Berns who wrote 'Twist and Shout' and produces the hits of Them, The Drifters, Solomon Burke, Ben E King and many other top flight R&B artists.

"Bert's new label 'Bang!' is already a smash in America, and I am happy to be able to form an association with him. Our first record on the label is 'Hang On Sloopy' by The McCoys. I have always believed the success of a record lies in two places, the mind and the feet. This one definitely leans towards feet and is one of the most infectious, danceable records I have heard in a long time with all the feel of a 'Twist and Shout' or 'Louie Louie'.

"Our second record is by a new group called Fifth Avenue produced by Jimmy Page. The song is the Pete Seeger folk classic 'The Bells of Rhymney'. The third record I produced myself. It features a very talented artist who you all saw on *Ready Steady Go!* a few weeks ago called Nico. Nico has recorded a great song by Gordon Lightfoot who composed the Peter, Paul and Mary smash 'For Loving Me'. Now Gordon had come up with a brand new song 'I'm Not Sayin'."

In an *NME* interview, the same week, Oldham expanded on his vision: "It is our policy to only put out releases that will be promoted by every means possible, contrary to the policy of the major labels in the country. We believe that success lies in dispensing with the accepted tradition and going against the current trend, which is to deal with pop merchandise in a stiff and unimaginative manner. We want to give an aura of youth. There's no room in business for an old-club atmosphere. One must adopt streamlined [US] methods of selling and promotion.

"The business has changed. Four years ago I was a fan when the big guys in blue suits dressed a kid in white and advertised him as a star. We believed in them. Today young people are setting the trend for kids of their own age. The group boom has broken every rule that applied to pop. What we're seeing is not just a musical phenomena, it's a social phenomenon."

On the evening of 20th August 1965 London's in-crowd were partying at Andrew Loog Oldham's behest. The venue he'd chosen was not one of the trendy, well-known club haunts, the Ad Lib, say. No, he was moving in much more exclusive circles than that. The Pickwick was a little publicised, well-to-do, refined night space cum restaurant, tucked away off the Charing Cross Road in Soho, more accustomed to hosting the higher echelons of the film industry than the new pop aristocracy. Owned by Wolf Mankowitz[17], a formidable writing ace of stage, screen and page. The 42-year-old is heavily involved in the Bond movie dynasty and an avuncular presence to young screen stars such as Terence Stamp, Michael Caine and Sean Connery.

---

17. Cyril Wolf Mankowitz (1924–1998) was an English writer, playwright and screenwriter particularly known for three novels - *Make Me an Offer* (1952), *A Kid for Two Farthings* (1953) and *My Old Man's a Dustman* - and many successful films. In 1962 Mankowitz introduced his friend Cubby Broccoli to Harry Saltzman, holder of the film rights to James Bond. Broccoli and Saltzman then formed Eon Productions and began co-producing the first Bond film, *Dr No*, for which Mankowitz was hired as one of the screenwriters. However after viewing early rushes Mankowitz feared that the film would be a disaster and damage his reputation and insisted on having his name be removed from the film's credits.

Mankowitz has had much luck turning his cockney-vérité novels into films and the 21 year-old Loog Oldham is telling anyone who'll listen how indebted he is to Wolf's fifties record biz satire, *Expresso Bongo*, the story of a sharp rock 'n' roll manager, 'Soho Johnny' played by Laurence Harvey, making and losing a star on the Tin Pan Alley[18]/ early Brit rock scene.

The Byrds, the first American group to have success with their own take on the Stones/Beatles led 'British Invasion', are all ears. They huddle round Oldham as he whispers conspiratorially behind the back of his hand, eyes hidden by dark glasses, telling them how he got the Stones a record deal at Decca in the first place: copying a stunt in *Expresso Bongo*. As he was sitting down to break bread with Dick Rowe, Head of A&R, he had a heel call the office to alert Dick to the fact they had an offer from a rival company (they hadn't but Oldham knew Rowe, who was infamous for turning down The Beatles, was terrified of turning down another hit group). Oldham turns to whisper into Mick Jagger's ear. Mick has heard enough about this film to last a lifetime. Jagger cackles though when Oldham tells him The Byrds might be worth stealing if they didn't all look like Brian, Mick is a bitch but Oldham is outrageous with it. Mick goes back to the sulk/slump cool pose and watches Oldham work the room. This is supposed to be the Stones' party too but as usual it's all about fucking Andrew!

Oldham feels safe stood with the two loud, savvy, New York ladies especially flown in for the evening. Out of the three, it is difficult to say who is the most ripped, made-up and fancifully dressed. Both women are called Linda and

---

18. This area of NY, specifically West 28th Street between Fifth and Sixth Avenues in the Flower District of Manhattan, was the accepted centre of the city's music publishing and songwriting world between 1885 and the 1930s. The phrase as it relates to the early rock 'n' roll period usually centres around the songwriters and publishers who coalesced in the Brill Building at 1619 Broadway.

Oldham needn't explain to either about *Expresso Bongo* or why Mick's got the hump.

Linda Stein is married to an upcoming Brill Building[19] kid called Seymour, who would become legend himself when he formed Sire Records in the 70s signing Madonna, Depeche Mode and Talking Heads. Linda would bring him The Ramones who she managed. The young couple steered Oldham to sign the contract with Bert Berns. Seymour is talking about James Brown signing for Immediate.

Then there is Linda Goldner, daughter of Red Bird biz legend George, currently working for Artie Ripp, head of New York's Kama Sutra Records, an indie that has inspired Oldham.

Marianne Faithfull and Oldham's latest discovery, ice queen Nico, lend the party a different layer of exoticism. They, along with Oldham's wife Sheila and Keith Richards' girlfriend Linda Keith (really) who is Sheila's best friend, are teasing the green Eric Clapton and teenage Jimmy Page, passing around a joint. Page is Calder's kid, an in-demand session guitarist. Calder also wants to sign Steve Marriott to Immediate and Marriott is tempted. Mickie Most[20] recognises the pungent smell and moves away. Oldham and Calder represent one of his main acts, Herman's Hermits, who are busy conquering America. Most is a rival of sorts

---

19. By 1962 the Brill Building contained 165 music businesses. A musician could find a publisher and a printer, cut a demo, promote the record and cut a deal with radio promoters, all within this one building. In this way professionals in the music business took control after rock and roll's first wave; there were no more unpredictable or rebellious singers, in fact a specific singer in most cases could be easily replaced with another. Songs were written to order by pros who could custom fit music and lyrics targeted at a teen audience.

20. Born Michael Peter Hayes (1938 – 2003), Most was an English record producer behind scores of hit singles for acts such as the Animals, Herman's Hermits, Donovan and Lulu, often issuing them on his own RAK Records label. ALO once told me he pissed on Mickie Most's Rolls Royce.

to Oldham, he has three No. 1 American singles under his belt with various acts and is a millionaire as a result. But he's 27. "27!" as Tom Wolfe[21] might say.

There's music and dancing but everyone stays cool, handsomely tailored, subtly illuminated. Wolf Mankowitz's son Gered, 21, newly appointed as successor to David Bailey as the Stones chief photographer, is working the room, snapping the cream of this new London society. The Who's managers, Kit Lambert[22] and Chris Stamp[23], keep offices in the same apartment block as Oldham and Calder and are eager to learn how they can fuck over the business and make their own millions. Pete Townshend shows his face but only lasts five minutes as speed and an early sniff of cocaine are already turning him inside out. Of the Stones: Keith is imperious; Charlie dapper; Bill on the pull and Brian shakes his blonde hair and grins leerily.

'Satisfaction' is already No. 1 in America, the band's

---

21. Thomas Kennerly Wolfe Jr. (1930 – 2018) was an American author and journalist widely known for his association with New Journalism, a style of news writing and journalism developed in the 1960s and 1970s that incorporated literary techniques

Wolfe experimented with four literary devices not normally associated with feature writing: scene-by-scene construction, extensive dialogue, multiple points of view, and detailed description of individuals' status-life symbols (the material choices people make). He later referred to this style as literary journalism. Of the use of status symbols, Wolfe has said, "I think every living moment of a human being's life, unless the person is starving or in immediate danger of death in some other way, is controlled by a concern for status.".

22. Christopher Sebastian Lambert (1935–1981) was the son of composer Constant Lambert and part-time actress Florence Kaye. His godmother was Margot Fonteyn, the prima ballerina who danced for Constant's company, the Royal Ballet, and with whom Constant had an affair causing him to leave Lambert's mother.

23. Christopher Thomas Stamp (1942–2012) was born into a working-class East End family. His father, Thomas Stamp, was a tugboat captain. His elder brother was noted actor and face of the sixties Terence Stamp.

first, and tomorrow it'll be released in Britain as a single simultaneously with the first three Immediate singles. Everyone at the party is quietly or loudly blown away by the track that was pulled out of the hat by Oldham or, if you prefer formalities, was 'Produced by Andrew Loog Oldham' as it trumpets on all the Stones' records.

It requires little hype from the man himself, so his focus is his new label. "Immediate is the most exciting thing for me since the Stones made their chart debut," he tells Mickie Most, as reported by *NME*.

The following day full-page adverts appeared in *NME*, *Melody Maker*, *Record Mirror*, and *Disc and Music Echo*, the four main music weeklies. It was over the top; at the time even new records by major acts, even the Stones, were afforded no more than a quarter page advert in these outlets. The graphic style, reliant on typography over images, became a distinct house style at Immediate.

BIG ROCKETS FLY HIGH; OUT OF REACH.

THEY CAN'T SEE YOU, NOR YOU THEM.

YOU CAN SEE SMALL ROCKETS

THEY CAN SEE YOU

THAT IS CONTACT!"

IMMEDIATE RECORDS

A NEW RECORD COMPANY OF TOMORROW

TODAY

'Satisfaction' shot to the top of the UK chart, brushing aside The Walker Brothers' 'Make It Easy On Yourself', becoming the Stones' fourth consecutive UK No. 1. With

the backing of pirate radio stations, London and Caroline,
The McCoys' 'Hang On Sloopy' became Immediate's first
hit. By early October the song had replaced 'Satisfaction'
at No. 1 on many charts. Already a No. 1 in the US, the
single was another first for the history books: a bi-coastal
independent chart-topper. The McCoys consisted of four
non-descript teens from the US; the youngest (a stand-up
drummer) was just 17. During the nine-week chart life of
'Hang On Sloopy', Immediate sold roughly 180,000 copies
of the single — a phenomenal start for the new label.
While The McCoys' bubblegum pop was the 'sound' of the
Immediate launch, the label's 'look' came courtesy of Nico,
who was ready and available for promotion in London
unlike the McCoys who were set to tour the UK later in
the year.

    The international fashion model had heard Oldham
was looking for girls "to turn into stars" after his success
with Marianne Faithfull. Nico, real name Christa Paffgen,
was German with long blonde hair and incredible bone
structure. It was easy to see why Brian Jones had fallen
for her when they met in Paris after a Stones show at the
Olympia. Years later Nico would document her relationship
with Jones in vivid, vicious terms: how he knocked her
around, leaving her bleeding and bruised, once trying to
pin a brooch to her vaginal lips, fucking her with a loaded
gun and pouring hot wax on her nipples. Nico could have
been using Jones to get to Oldham, who was impressed
enough by her modelling credentials, film work in Fellini's
La Dolce Vita, and friendship with Bob Dylan, to give her a
first recording break. Oldham remembers signing Nico to a
deal in LA while recording 'Satisfaction'.

    In Richard Witts' book, *Nico, The Life and Lies of an
Icon*, she claimed that Oldham took her to a secluded toilet
where they each snorted a line of high-grade speed and
Nico recalled him saying: "It's time to do a deal. I'm going
to start up a Rolling Stones record company. They'll be

the producers and so will I, and we'll be able to give the breaks to people we love, like you, Nico. Once we've got the business sorted out with the legal people there'll be a contract for you. I'm thinking three singles for a start."

Originally Nico had wanted to record the song Dylan had written for her, 'I'll Keep It With Mine' but Oldham considered the sentiment and tempo too downbeat for a debut. Brian Jones reassured a disappointed Nico not to worry and that his manager, Oldham, "knew the trade inside out". Nico wondered what trade he meant. "The drugs trade I think," she told Witts.

After recording her singing a cover of Dylan's 'Blowin' in the Wind', a track he had already cut with Marianne Faithfull on vocals, Oldham cherry-picked Gordon Lightfoot's, 'I'm Not Sayin'' for Nico's Immediate debut. Lightfoot[24] had already written hits for Elvis Presley, Johnny Cash, and Barbra Streisand and was managed by Albert Grossman (who was also Bob Dylan's manager).

Three months before her twenty-eighth birthday Nico was the oldest person present at the recording at Regent Sound, the basement demo studio in Denmark Street, Soho's 'Tin Pan Alley', where Oldham had also cut his first Stones hits. Assembled as backing for Nico were Brian Jones and Oldham's regular guitar/bass duo (and future Led Zeppelin band mates) Jimmy Page and John Paul Jones plus Oldham's preferred arranger Art Greenslade who down-pitched the backing, allowing the mono-toned Nico to half chant, half curse her way through the lyrics. Oldham jotted down some downcast lyrics for the b-side, 'The Last Mile', which Page quickly shaped into a passable song and recorded.

---

24. Gordon Meredith Lightfoot Jr (1938 – 2023) was a Canadian singer-songwriter and guitarist. Bob Dylan said of him, "I can't think of any Gordon Lightfoot song I don't like. Every time I hear a song of his, it's like I wish it would last forever."

Nico appeared on (the then live) *Ready Steady Go!* but it turned into a disaster. Her timing was out and the band and orchestra, conducted by Art Greenslade, were only half way done by the time she had finished the lyric. Still, her stunning looks, exotic European accent and vacant pose were a hit with the press and photos of her —sometimes happily posing with Oldham and Calder — were valuable publicity for Immediate.

In a promotional film she was filmed lip-syncing to 'I'm Not Sayin', swaying and pouting by the River Thames, but chart success proved elusive and when Brian Jones introduced her to Andy Warhol she jumped ship. Warhol took 'I'm Not Sayin'' as her *de facto* audition for Factory and would soon launch her alongside The Velvet Underground.

Oldham told me he didn't bear her any grudges because, as Immediate took its first strides, personalities were what the label required and Nico notably had been one of them. "We served each other well for those few minutes in 1965 when she allowed us to unsuccessfully emulate the advanced copy of [Bob Lind's] 'Elusive Butterfly'[25] we had and some of the stellar Jackie DeShannon[26] demos we loved. The McCoys with 'Hang On Sloopy' went to No. 1 for us but were unavailable and ugly. Nico[27] helped us promote ourselves, and she understood the rhythm of life,

---

25 'Elusive Butterfly' was written and performed by American folk singer Bob Lind (1942-) and released as a single in December 1965 reaching No.5 in both the US and UK charts in the spring of 1966.
26 Jackie DeShannon (born Sharon Lee Myers, August 21, 1941) is an American singer-songwriter best known as the singer of 'What the World Needs Now Is Love' and 'Put a Little Love in Your Heart'.
27. Born in Berlin into the wealthy Päffgen Kölsch master brewer family dynasty, Nico (1938-88) was evacuated out of Berlin to escape WWII. Heroin addiction and a career downturn led her to spend her final years in Prestwich, Manchester. For a few months in the 1980s she had shared an apartment in Brixton with Salford punk poet John Cooper Clarke.

did the movie and moved on to the next part."

When he had agreed to join as Staff Producer', 'little' Jimmy Page, 21, was already one of the top session guitarists on the London recording scene. He had been nicknamed 'little Jimmy' so as not be confused with 'Big' Jim Sullivan, the other, older, pre-eminent session guitarist of the time. Oldham had used both Jims on many past recordings, including on his super-groovy Andrew Loog Oldham Orchestra jam albums. Oldham often paired Page with bassist John Baldwin who he re-named John Paul Jones. Like Page, Oldham gave Jones a leg-up, promoting him to arranger. Jones was forever grateful. At the time Oldham said of Page, "he's exceptionally talented" with "a big career ahead".

Page and Calder became especially close. The pair had been on a wild LA trip together, checking in at independent label Liberty Records (who had released 'Elusive Butterfly'). Page was also a fan of Liberty's new act, Jackie DeShannon, who had scored a huge hit in the US with 'Needles and Pins'. He wrote the song 'Come Stay With Me' for her, a song that, back in the UK, Calder recorded with Marianne Faithfull (for contractual reasons, Faithfull stayed with Decca and was never an Immediate act).

For his first Immediate single Page took vocal duo Fifth Avenue into the studio to harmonise over his guitar on a cover of the Pete Seeger[28] written 'The Bells of Rhymney'. The Byrds had covered the same song as the centrepiece for their debut album and the sound of the Immediate single was almost identical. Page 'arranged, produced and conducted' the release and wrote the 'moody' (he said) b-side, 'Just Like Anyone Would Do', with a sweet recurring

---

28. Peter Seeger (May 3, 1919 – January 27, 2014) was an American folk singer and social who was blacklisted during the McCarthy era but rose to prominence during the folk revival of the early 60s penning chart-topping records such as 'If I Had a Hammer' and 'Turn! Turn! Turn!'.

guitar motif. Questioned about the single over a decade later by 1970s rock magazine *Trouser Press*, Page said: "It's got a fantastic sound on it. I used a double pick-up on the acoustic guitar; it had nice Beach Boys type harmonies. The band was just session musicians that happened to be around."

Calder: "Everything Jimmy Page wanted to do for Immediate we let him. He was a lovely fella. His mum used to ring up our office and say, 'Is my Jimmy there?' She would be at home waiting up for him."

I Want Work

Over the final months of 1965, Immediate released 20 more singles by an odd ragbag of artists in a bewildering diversity of styles. Page produced a Liverpudlian outfit, The Masterminds[29], who were discovered by Oldham after a Stones gig in the city. They created a passable homage cover of Bob Dylan's 'She Belongs To Me'. Calder then hooked Page up with teenage psychedelic outfit Les Fleurs de Lys[30] for a cute cover of Buddy Holly's 'Moondreams', Page writing the B-side 'Wait For Me'. Oldham chipped in with a great everything-but-the-kitchen-sink production of a Kennedy Street Enterprises act, The Factotums[31], on a cover of a track he

---

29. Originally formed in 1963 The Masterminds have been described as "one of the more promising late-era Merseybeat bands who never managed to translate their potential into serious record sales". By late 1964 they had established a successful residency at the Blue Angel club when one night ALO saw them performing Bob Dylan songs. However despite an appearance on *Ready! Steady! Go!* the resulting single sank without a trace, along with the group's prospects for breaking out of Liverpool. Joey Molland later found success with Badfinger.

30. Originally formed in late 1964, in Southampton, Les Fleur de Lys were a freakbeat band before disbanding in 1969. However keyboardist Pete Sears went on to play on four early Rod Stewart albums, while bassist Gordon Haskell replaced Greg Lake in King Crimson.

31. Formed in Audenshaw, Manchester as a beat group, The Factotums adopted Beach Boy style harmonies. After signing them, ALO changed their image and recorded them for Decca before a fallout led to the recordings being lost and the band signed to Immediate. The Factotums career stalled when their second single 'You're So Good To Me' failed to gain sufficient radio play.

had heard on an Ivy League single, 'In My Lonely Room';
writing his own piss-take b-side for the release, 'A Run In
The Green And Tangerine Flaked Forest'.

The Yardbirds production team, Giorgio Gomelsky
and Paul Samwell-Smith, directed the release of another
Kennedy Street act, The Mockingbirds, who were
managed by Herman's Hermits manager, Harvey Lisberg.
Their haunting single 'You Stole My Love' was written by
their lead singer, 19-year-old Graham Gouldman, who
had already written massive hits for The Yardbirds ('For
Your Love' — a US Top 10 entry) and The Hollies ('Look
Through Any Window').

There was the bubblegum beat of 'Cara-Lin' by The
Strangeloves[32] courtesy of Bert Berns' Bang! label. Also
from the US, via a deal with Hercules Records, came the
Dylan pastiche, 'Down And Out' by Joey Levine[33], who
would go on to front acts for bubblegum label Buddha,
and Barbara Lynn's smallish cult R&B hit 'You Can't Buy
Me Love' through a deal with Jamie Records. In the early
1960s Lynn[34] had a hit US No. 1 as an 18-year-old with
her R&B classic, 'You'll Lose a Good Thing' and she was

---

32. The Strangeloves were created in 1964 by the New York-based
American songwriting and production team of Bob Feldman, Jerry
Goldstein, and Richard Gottehrer. Before the invention of The
Strangeloves, Feldman and Goldstein had been working together as
songwriters since 1959. Deciding that they could not convincingly
fake British accents, they opted to pretend to be Australians. Publicity
material issued about the group claimed the band were three brothers
named Giles, Miles, and Niles Strange who were raised on an
Australian sheep farm.

33. Joey Levine sang lead vocals on several Top 40 singles including
'Yummy Yummy Yummy', although he is more famous as the writer
of advertising jingles such as 'Just For the Taste of It – Diet Coke' and
'This Bud's For You'.

34. Unusually for the mid-60s, Lynn was a female African American
singer who both wrote most of her own songs and played a lead
instrument.

a Stones favourite; they had recorded another of her hits 'Oh Baby (We Got a Good Thing Goin')'.

Kinks and Who producer Shel Talmy[35] recorded Van Lenton's single 'Gotta Get Away', a Cilla Black-style easy-listening outing. There was also The Golden Apples of the Sun, a group supposedly managed by photographer David Bailey and fronted by a girl with great pipes. Oldham produced their cover of Curtis Mayfield's 'Monkey Time'.

Teenager Greg Phillips had been dropped in Oldham's lap by his show business pal Lionel Bart. As a 14-year-old he starred in a film[36] with Dirk Bogarde and Judy Garland, and the latter had become a sort of surrogate mother to Phillips in London. Phillips was friends with another former child actor, Steve Marriott, and, over the past few years had cut a few singles for Pye between acting jobs. Page and Oldham co-produced a single for Phillips, a cover of Billy Joe Royal's version of 'Down in the Boondocks', a US smash that Oldham was led to believe would not be given a release in the UK. However, a few weeks after Immediate put out Phillips' version, the original was made available in the UK and Greg lost the chart battle.

"Folk plus protest equal hits," Oldham noted in one of his final *Disc and Music Echo* columns, as Dylan, The Byrds and Barry McGuire's 'Eve Of Destruction' rose to the top of the US charts. Immediate signed Mick Softly, a folk-styled songwriter friend of Donovan ("Britain's Dylan"), and released his single 'I'm So Confused', produced by

---

35. Born in Chicago, Talmy moved to LA and became a recording engineer for TV before turning to music. Before he went on an extended holiday to Europe in 1962 a friend handed him some acetates and told him to pass them off as his own. Gaining an interview with Dick Rowe of Decca he played the records and was immediately offered a job as an independent producer. A year later Talmy recorded 'You Really Got Me' for The Kinks, credited as the first recording to feature heavy metal chords.
36. *I Could Go On Singing* (1963)

Donovan's managers, Geoff Stephens and Peter Eden.
Immediate's press releases were often as entertaining as their
records, and for his Dylan impersonating release, Softly was
suggested to have been a Jesuit novice who now insisted on
wearing a monk's habit on all television appearances. The
song was billed 'the record America refused to release'.

Immediate also pressed up the Julian Protest Quintet's
instrumental version of 'Satisfaction', with a comical b-side
written by Oldham, 'Like A Bob Dylan' in response to
Dylan's breakthrough cut, 'Like A Rolling Stone'. More
laughs came courtesy of comic Jimmy Tarbuck, the new
MC on ITV's top show *Sunday Night At The London Palladium*.
Oldham took him into the studio with Art Greenslade
arranging to produce a cover of the Ricky Nelson hit,
'Someday (You'll Want Me To Want You)', a big band
version of which he had seen Cher perform. The b-side
of the Tarbuck single was a Jagger/Richards song, 'We're
Wasting Time'. Greenslade recalled: "It was Jimmy
Tarbuck's first record, I went in and he was absolutely
crapping his pants, he was so scared."

Another Mick and Keith song, 'So Much In Love', was
used as an a-side for an act called Charles Dickens, fronted
by fashion photographer, David Anthony. Stones recording
engineer Glyn Johns went from control booth to vocal
booth for his debut single, a deep-voiced croon cover of
The Shadows recent hit 'Mary-Anne'. Unfortunately, sales
of the single were less than the number of promotional
copies sent to press and radio.

The McCoys finally arrived in London to promote their
'Hang On Sloopy' follow-up, 'Fever', and their debut UK
album, *The McCoys*. A ten-day visit included performances
on *Ready Steady Go!* and *Top of the Pops* however 'Fever' was a
little too cabaret-inspired but the b-side 'Sorrow' was later a
top five hit for The Merseys. Later still, David Bowie would
cover the same song on his *Pin Ups* (1973) album.

Oldham had established a relationship with The Poets

from Glasgow in 1964 after he'd eloped to marry his teenage girlfriend Sheila Klein. John Lennon had been a huge fan of his early productions of the band (all released by Decca), and now the group recorded their debut Immediate single 'Call Again'. Oldham enjoyed their droning sound and the fact that they performed original material, the stark simplicity of which afforded him a lot of space in which to indulge his Phil Spector doppelgänger, with reverb and additional percussion to the fore. Poets' singer George Gallagher recalled "wide boy trickster" Tony Calder handing out the group's £8 a week Immediate wage.

Immediate also raided Soho's trendy Hammond and horns urban R&B scene (the UK's hottest underground movement) and signed up two of the leading lights, John Mayall and Chris Farlowe. Both were regulars at the Flamingo Club on Wardour Street, home to wild crowds of mods, jazzers, US servicemen, prostitutes and pimps; all getting their kicks to a steamy mix of Blue Note, Jamaican Blue Beat, American Stax and Tamla Motown music.

Mancunian guitarist and singer/songwriter John Mayall had made a name for himself in London with his Bluesbreakers outfit featuring Eric Clapton on guitar and Jack Bruce on bass — men who later became two thirds of supergroup Cream - and was managed by Rik Gunnell who also ran the Flamingo Club and had a reputation for being tough and enterprising. Gunnell was building a stable of credible blues talent: Chris Farlowe, Alan Price (who had just left The Animals), Geno Washington and The Shotgun Express.

John Mayall & the Bluesbreakers recorded the evil, horror-inspired, 'I'm Your Witchdoctor' for Immediate. Written by Mayall and produced by Jimmy Page, the song is an outstanding example of sixties' British blues at its best, sounding like Jimi Hendrix several years in advance.

At first glance Chris Farlowe was a rat-faced Mod, but on stage he was loud and powerful. Otis Redding apparently rated him and he arrived at Immediate with his own hot backing group, The Thunderbirds, featuring Albert Lee on guitar and Nicky Hopkins on piano. Farlowe had been a regular on the Hamburg scene in the early 1960s before signing to Gunnell and had already recorded for Decca, EMI and Sue, but, aged 25, was still looking for his first hit. However his EMI single 'Buzz With The Fuzz' had won him many Mod admirers, including Paul McCartney, Steve Winwood and Georgie Fame. Animals vocalist Eric Burdon was also a Farlowe fan and the pair performed together on an episode of *Ready Steady Go!* devoted to the music of Otis Redding. Burdon was persuaded in to the studio to produce Farlowe's debut single for Immediate, 'The Fool'.

Oldham praised Farlowe in the *NME*, saying: "He's the first since Mick Jagger who can really sing and, with the right pushing, he could become not only an R&B singer but an all-round entertainer." Jagger was also a fan and, toward the end of 1965, the Stones singer went public with his involvement at Immediate, announcing he had become Farlowe's new producer, along with Oldham and Keith Richards under the guise of 'We Three Producers'. At IBC studios, with Art Greenslade arranging, they cut a four-track EP entitled *In The Midnight Hour* which featured the title track plus covers of 'Mr Pitiful', 'Satisfaction' and an obscure Anthony Newley[37] track 'Who Can I Turn To?'. Despite the EP retailing at almost double the price of a single, it made No.21 in the singles chart, and No. 1 on the EP charts.

Immediate's final release of 1965 was a Christmas single produced by a teenage Gary Glitter, then going by the name of Paul Raven (real name Paul Gadd), and

---

37. Anthony Newley (1931–1999) was an English actor, singer, songwriter, and filmmaker described as a "latter-day British Al Jolson" who achieved widespread success scoring a dozen entries on the UK Top 40 chart and writing hits such as 'Goldfinger'. He married Joan Collins in 1963 but they divorced 7 years later.

advertised as being 'Ski Sound'. It was The Variations covering Brian Wilson's 'The Man With All The Toys', a track taken from *The Beach Boys Christmas Album*. Rounding off the year, Immediate took out more full-page music press ads to simply wish the UK record industry a "Merry Christmas".

In the *NME* end of year round-up issue, 'Whiter Shade Of Pale' recording manager Denny Cordell named Oldham as "definitely Mr 1965", saying, "he has built the Rolling Stones supremely, successfully-launched a promising new label, Immediate, and adds great atmosphere at recording sessions". Decca Promotions manager Tony Hall, rounding up his year in *Record Mirror,* gave "full hallmarks for the one and only Andrew Oldham, who has consistently enlivened (if often infuriated) the record business this year — under the frighteningly astute guidance of Allen Klein — and who had the guts to start Britain's first real independent label".

I asked Oldham if he could elaborate on some of these early Immediate releases but he merely pointed to his hectic late 1965 schedule with the Stones. US accountant Allen Klein was renegotiating the Stones' deal with Decca, as 'Get Off Of My Cloud' followed 'Satisfaction' to No. 1 in the US and UK charts (their fifth consecutive UK No. 1, equalling the tally of Elvis and The Beatles). The "wonderful pressure of success", as Oldham called it, was "relentless". The most time-consuming aspect of Oldham's year was a Klein-arranged mammoth end of 1965 US tour covering 35 cities in six-weeks to clinch the Stones arrival in the top league of US entertainers, grossing them a massive $1.5 million.

Oldham was also working overtime to facilitate the growing demands for Stones' product in the US patching together an album, *December's Children (And Everybody's)* and a single, 'As Tears Go By', for the Christmas market. In the UK a new album *Out of Our Heads* topped the charts.

There were also five *Top of the Pops* and three *Ready Steady Go!* appearances to oversee — including a *Ready Steady Go! Rolling Stones Special*, on which Oldham and Jagger performed a duet on Sonny and Cher's 'I Got You Babe'.

With Calder largely left at the Immediate wheel — and excluding 'Hang On Sloopy' and the Stones-promoted Chris Farlowe EP — none of these early Immediate singles troubled the Top 20. Calder explained to me how, at the time, "working a record" was a case of testing the waters with radio DJs by sending out promos and, if nobody was keen, just moving on to the next. He said he had encouraged this turnover of singles and acts to "try and establish ourselves".

Calder could pursue this policy partly due to the innovative deal Immediate had with Philips, who paid for the manufacturing and distribution of Immediate records in return for a 17.5 per cent share of profits: payment every 30 days on records sold. The Stones, for instance, had been forced to wait 18 long months before getting their first royalties from Decca.

The structure of the Philips deal meant there was a constant feed of Immediate money (chiefly from 'Hang on Sloopy') with which Calder could work.

There's no question that Calder's tactics were successful, even if Oldham would have preferred another hit. The deluge of weird early singles had given the label cult appeal. Alongside the No. 1 straight out of the trap and the hard-to-ignore adverts, Immediate felt established.

The first full-time employee at the new company was Tony King, hired by Oldham to work alongside Calder as Immediate's new Head of Promotions. In his early 20s, King had already racked up an impressive CV, working at Decca in promotions and as a personal assistant to Roy Orbison. Despite the 138/147 Ivor Court address suggesting a suite of offices, King[38] worked from Oldham's office at 138 where the Stones business affairs were administered and Calder worked out of 147, a floor above. Nonetheless Ivor Court was a ritzy residential apartment block near Baker Street, overlooking Regent's Park. Both offices were rented for £50 a week.

The Immediate 'engine room', with its black and white tiled floor, was Calder's office, where he lived with his girlfriend Josie. Oldham's office was seen as more creative. One interviewer noted Oldham, in 138, "poised on a chair he had had made to spec for £80", curtains drawn, decked out in tight 'sludge-green' corduroys, suede Clark's desert boots, a 'pyjama-style' striped shirt with a chunky silver identity bracelet, 'long blonde hair curling over a tan suede jacket'. Here, the marijuana leaf wallpaper was complimented by brown and green velvet décor. It was a good bolthole in central London, everyone concurred, and King recalls often arriving at 138 to find Keith Richards or other acts asleep in the bedroom.

Tony King: "I worked hard promoting 'Hang On Sloopy', pulling in favours. We weren't in it for the money, it was just fun. I did all the mailing myself, I did all the packing of the envelopes. I had a tiny office and I was

---

38. After Immediate, King was approached by Sir George Martin's independent production company to promote for artists such as Cilla Black, The Hollies, Manfred Mann, Tom Jones, and The Beatles. In 1970 he joined Apple as general manager and he later pulled together the album *Ringo* which went to No.1 and he was asked to stay on to do the same thing for John Lennon's *Mind Games*. When Apple closed in 1976 King became Executive VP of Elton John's label, Rocket, and later became Head of Club Promotion for RCA, which was followed two years later by a move to Creative Director for RCA. In 1984 Mick Jagger hired King work on his first solo album, *She's The Boss* and he stayed with Mick, and subsequently The Stones, for the next 27 years. In 2011 he joined Elton John's team, initially working on his Las Vegas show, *The Million Dollar Piano*, and then working on his albums and world tour.

just furiously stuffing envelopes full of records, sticking on stamps and taking them to the post office, running around town delivering them to the BBC. I loved doing it. I would do it until midnight or 2am. There was a lot of pot [marijuana] around. I was the official pot holder. I had to go around the corner to these two call girls who always had really good stuff, and I would keep different types of grass in different drawers in the office.

"Tony's job was to whip up the troops,' King added. "He used to piss people off most of the time. Once he was shouting, 'I want work!' Oldham and I burst out laughing and it became a sort of catchphrase in the office. Tony was important to Oldham but Oldham was dismissive toward him much of the time. He thought of him as a good joke. Tony was hard-edged, hard-nosed in business; he could be Oldham's bad guy. When there was dirty work to be done Tony could do it and Oldham would still look okay."

All Mick

After prising Chris Farlowe away from the constraints of his backing group, The Thunderbirds, Immediate set about making him the label's first official 'star'. Pop music and teen culture was not really Farlowe's bag, but he was smartly dressed and, from certain angles, looked pretty sharp. Covering 'Satisfaction' on the recent Jagger/Richards/Oldham produced EP had given Farlowe a taste of what was to come. On his new Immediate single he covered the Jagger/Richards song, 'Think', which the Stones had recently recorded in Hollywood for inclusion on an album in the making. For extra kudos Jagger sang backing vocals on the single and was named as the single's sole producer. The explosive, trumpet-driven single was swiftly followed by a debut album, *14 Things To Think About*, made up of an old mix of Thunderbirds-backed blues and soul standards and more modern touches such as covers of Dylan's 'It's All Over Now, Baby Blue' and The Beatles' 'Yesterday'.

In an early January 1966 edition of *Melody Maker* Farlowe was photographed for the cover with his manager, Rik Gunnell, who was holding a gun to his head, as a new contract with Gunnell Management was signed. The paper reported Farlowe was guaranteed £50,000 (from Immediate) over the next five years, one of the era's first big buck deals — and everyone understood Gunnell was not a man to be messed with when it came to cash. Oldham now had money to burn after Allen Klein had extracted £600,000 from Decca to extend the label's relationship with the Stones for two more years. Klein also bandied about the phenomenal figure of £5 million in future guarantees.

Oldham was declared a "paper millionaire".

The Stones manager added a new motor to his car fleet, which already including a Chevy, a Lincoln and a maroon Sunbeam Tiger convertible with V8 engine, buying a gleaming £19,000 black Rolls Royce Phantom 5. Oldham was only the third British owner of this top of the range motor after John Lennon and HM The Queen. It came with blacked-out windows, a telephone, a record player and a bar.

However Oldham's violent psychopath chauffeur, Reg 'the Butcher' King, would not get to enjoy the Rolls Royce, having just received a five-year driving ban. The Butcher's final act of madness was mowing down scores of Stones' fans while reversing Oldham and the group away from a crazed crowd waiting backdoor after a gig. Oldham's new chauffeur, Eddie Reed, would be ever-present for the rest of the decade but would never disclose what he saw at the wheel of the Phantom.

Gunnell told *Melody Maker* about his dealings with Immediate: "Oldham came to me and said he wanted to record John Mayall. I said, 'Okay, but take Chris because he's a great talent and I'm going to develop him'." Farlowe recalled singing at Gunnell's Flamingo Club while Oldham worked the bar as a 16-year-old in the early 1960s and now thought it "a little bit weird" to be working for him. "Mind you," he added, "he knows what he is doing." Oldham rounded off the backslapping in the press when he said: "That man [Farlowe] is so humble. It's refreshing to find someone who retains an air of humility after being helped."

Farlowe's second Immediate single, 'Think', sold a respectable 23,000 copies in its first week but its failure to break the Top 20 had both Oldham and Jagger spitting feathers in the press about the way the British charts were compiled, implying there was either a fix or conspiracy. Jagger's heavy involvement upped the stakes for Immediate and Farlowe's next recording was a cover of the Jagger/

Richards classic 'Out Of Time', a song which, like 'Think', they had cut during the new album sessions in Hollywood, but one perhaps good enough to have been a Stones single. Adverts for Farlowe's 'Out Of Time' featured a photo of Jagger draping an arm round the singer, with Mick's involvement as producer heavily strap-lined.

Oldham's regular arranger, Art Greenslade, who was also working with The Kinks, Dusty Springfield, Shirley Bassey, Johnny Halliday and Serge Gainsborough, told me: "My first big hit with Immediate was Chris Farlowe's 'Out Of Time'... We went in and did the track but Mick couldn't get Chris's voice on it. I stopped up at Immediate later and Andrew said, 'Well, Art what do you think of this?' He had taken Chris Farlowe in and done it. Andrew must have worked hard in there, Chris Farlowe couldn't sing his way out of a paper bag. I'm sure Andrew must have done it, where you get an artist singing and you can do a sentence at a time, stitching it all together. He must have done it in pieces."

Tony Calder: "They all thought 'Out Of Time' was a b-side. I told Andrew, 'That's an a-side'. He said, 'No, you do as I tell you'. I said, 'Okay' and just took the tapes and put it out. When it went to No.1, Mick gave this interview about how long they had spent working on it and how it was all Mick's idea. That to me was the real introduction to how great artists really are."

Tony King: "It was fucking hard work; it didn't go to No. 1 by itself. We were very lucky; we got a hell of a lot of radio and television because it was Mick and Keith's song. We got Mick and Keith to do backing vocals on *Ready Steady Go!* They wrote it, produced it and promoted it. There was a great Gered Mankowitz snap of Jagger and Farlowe in the adverts, possibly there was a fleet of cars dashing around to crucial shops buying up records."

Two hundred thousand sales of 'Out Of Time' gave Immediate their second No. 1 hit. Tony Calder told the

BBC that Mick Jagger and Keith Richards — although unsure about their newly acquired roles at Immediate — were definitely on board. "I told them," he said, "if we say you can do it, you can do it!".

Jagger announced he was taking exclusive control of recording Farlowe. The relationship produced another single, Farlowe again covering a Jagger/Richards original 'Ride On Baby', recorded by the Stones during what were now being called the Hollywood *Aftermath* album sessions, but not included on the LP. It was another Top 20 hit and Farlowe told the press the production was "all Mick", but it was actually credited as "an Andrew Loog Oldham Production".

The "Mick Jagger produced" album that followed, *The Art Of Chris Farlowe*, reportedly cost a then wildly extravagant £17,000 to make. Farlowe admitted he didn't really have a hand in choosing the songs at Immediate, recalling: "Mick was involved with Immediate and it was a natural thing for him to get involved musically in the production side of things. When he was producing my album, Ike and Tina Turner did the backing vocals on 'North, South, East and West'."

The sleeve notes for *The Art Of Chris Farlowe*, written by Oldham (whose writings[39] were frequently a feature on Stones' albums) stated: "*The Art of Chris Farlowe* is now apparent and the emergence of Mick Jagger, the singer, as Jagger, the producer, has come from the combination of Farlowe's singing talent and both Jagger's rapport and communication with his public, and his growing understanding of today's sound. The songwriting team of Jagger and Richards; the arrangements of Art Greenslade, under the mind of Jagger, has finally given Chris Farlowe the recognition he deserves with two big hits behind him.

39. Oldham's often violent sleevenotes, cryptic poems and PR puff have never been collated but were dubbed by one wag as 'Loogalese'

We are proud to present his second album with Immediate; proud of Chris Farlowe, the artists, and Mick Jagger, the producer, and proud of this album that speaks for itself: so listen to *The Art of Chris Farlowe*."

Oldham and Jagger promoted the album together, conducting interviews at the trendy Trattoria Terrazzo restaurant in Soho where Oldham's movie idol, Laurence Harvey, and crooner Frank Sinatra (when he was in town) often ate. Despite their efforts it only sold about five thousand copies in the UK, enough to take it in to the Top 20 but hardly the sensation everybody anticipated.

"Andrew doesn't interfere but I accept his advice on sessions as he would accept mine on a Rolling Stones session," Jagger told the press. The situation with the Stones and Immediate gave Oldham the chance to push any talents Mick and Keith had. "From pissing to producing," he said.

Solo Keith

A first for any Beatle or Rolling Stone was Keith Richards' debut solo album, *Todays Pop Symphony*, a "new conception of today's hits in classical style" ran the blurb for what was being billed as "The Aranbee Pop Orchestra under the direction of Keith Richard".

Richards had gone cold on recording under the title of "The Keith Richard Orchestra", as everybody at Immediate had originally wanted. Oldham had a huge soft spot for Keith who, as a Rolling Stone, was often left in the shadow of Jagger and Jones. It was Oldham who had, in the band's early days, purposefully knocked the 's' off Keith's surname, doing so because he hoped he might be thought to be related to Cliff Richard. Shortly after this debut solo album the 's' was reinstated and Richards sailed forevermore.

"Directed and produced" by Keith, *Todays Pop Symphony* featured string-laden rock and orchestral versions of several Jagger/Richards originals, including 'Play With Fire', 'Mother's Little Helper', 'Sittin' on a Fence', and 'Take It or Leave It' plus similar styled versions of The Four Seasons' 'Rag Doll', Sonny and Cher's 'I Got You Babe', two Beatles numbers - 'There's a Place" and 'We Can Work It Out' plus 'In the Midnight Hour' and 'I Don't Want To Go On Without You' by Bert Berns and Jerry Wexler.

The cover featured a cartoon of Richards alongside Mozart, Beethoven, The Beatles, and Sonny and Cher, with a handsome photograph of Keith on the back. "If anyone thinks Keith's talents are limited, they will be forced to think again," Oldham told the press. "It's just something I've always wanted to do," admitted the Stones' guitarist. "He's just trying to prove he's a musician not just a rock 'n' roll guitarist," added Mick.

Oldham's sleevenotes for the album read: "Everybody in the pop industry is involved in the quick racket of hit records; a song comes and weeks later it is forgotten. But in a span of hits, regardless of the opinion of the so-called experts, great songs are written and should be remembered for they stand up on their own on any field against any competition. Here is a selection of today's hits in a stimulating album conceived by Rolling Stone, Keith Richard, who displays an outstanding sympathy and understanding for both his own art form and that of the classics and blends the two together in a great marriage of song and sound. This is an album that Immediate are proud to be associated with, a compliment to the industry that has been so good to us."

The album reached a respectable No.11 but there were doubts over the validity of Richards' involvement. This was a time when Jagger, Richards and Oldham were very close and had been dubbed the "unholy trinity" by the rest of the Stones. In his autobiography, *Stone Alone*, Bill Wyman wrote how he "always doubted that Keith had anything to do with its production or instigation". Adding: "I think it was probably Oldham's idea and execution, purely an Oldham projection of Keith to promote the album and to boost his public image, yet another round in Oldham's campaign to increase Keith's profile."

Oldham maintained that Richards planned and produced *Today's Pop Symphony* and didn't consider it important, nor does he remember who originated the idea. Recorded in a two-day session at IBC studios, engineered by Glyn Johns and arranged by Mike Leander, it sounded like a stringed-out version of the Andrew Loog Oldham Orchestra, whose three albums to date had been largely made up of surging orchestral rock arrangements of Oldham's favourite pop songs, often those of the Stones.

Keith's album was followed by the first UK posthumous album release of soul legend Sam Cooke who had recently been shot dead[40]. The sleeve of *The Wonderful World of Sam Cooke* came plastered with plaudits from Jagger, Richards, Eric Burdon, Georgie Fame, Roger Daltrey. Alan Freeman and many more. Oldham, who had been a fan since acting as PR on the 1962 Don Arden-promoted Cooke/Little Richard UK package tour, wrote: "This album is dedicated to the talent of the late great Sam Cooke, who was taken from us a little over a year ago, at just the starting point of his career. This album explains his roots, his affinity to the church, his source of inspiration for the great songs he wrote that have thrilled millions through his own performances and through the countless versions by countless artists in every language, in every country. The whole world has warmed to his joy, his sadness, and his conviction. This album is not a collection of his commercial outings but from the private collection of Allen Klein, who directed his career. It is released as a family tree, it enables us to trace back to Sam's roots, to his beginning of that fruitful tree that was taken from the earth in its spring. Sam was a rare leader, a rare quality in our industry of followers. I am proud to have been inspired by his warmth, talent and feel."

The album, made up of obscure Cooke material, went Top 20. The recordings had been gifted to Immediate by Oldham's new Stones business manager Allen Klein whose company, ABKCO, still owns Sam Cooke's astonishing back catalogue of hits. Klein, having just scored the Stones a massive new mega-bucks deal with Decca, was becoming

---

40. Cooke was killed at the age of 33 on December 11, 1964 at the Hacienda Motel, in South Central Los Angeles, California. Answering separate reports of a shooting and a kidnapping at the motel, police found Cooke's body. He had sustained a gunshot wound to the chest, which was later determined to have pierced his heart.

an increasingly influential figure in the lives of many UK acts. He controlled producer Mickie Most's recordings (Herman's Hermits, The Animals and Donovan) and was now 'in' with The Kinks and Marianne Faithfull. Klein secured Oldham over-rides on Faithfull's work for the US, and it briefly looked as if she would be leaving Decca and joining Immediate with Oldham taking "executive control". Oldham bought Faithfull a Mini as a sweetener and, while he was at it, bought a specially built Mini replica of the Phantom 5 for himself. Faithfull told the press: "I am happy to return to the fold. I like and have a very high regard for Andrew."

Klein also helped Immediate get a distribution deal in the US for Chris Farlowe's 'Out Of Time' with major label MGM and was looking to secure Immediate rights on MGM product in the UK (it was rumoured Bob Dylan was about to join MGM). As well as administering Sam Cooke's music publishing in the US, Klein was also in negotiations to buy Cameo Parkway, Roulette Records boss Morris Levy's Philadelphia label (Levy[41] was long suspected of being a member of the Mafia).

When Farlowe's 'Out Of Time' was released in America one of Klein's promotional men had got his dates mixed up; done his job too well. He had reported high distributor and radio station activity to chart compilers *Billboard*, *Cashbox* and *Record World* when the record wasn't yet available! There were a lot of red faces at Immediate and two weeks later, when 'Out Of Time' was pressed, a lot

---

41. Born Moishe Levy (1927–1990). Upon his death Levy was described by *Billboard* magazine as "one of the record industry's most controversial and flamboyant players" and by *Variety* as "The Octopus", for his far-reaching control, disproportionate to the size of his companies, in every area of the record business. It is alleged that Levy falsely took writing credit in order to receive royalties, enriching himself at the expense of many of his signed artists, especially black R&B artists.

of stations were afraid to touch the record in case it looked like they'd been bought.

With suspicions that the Mafia were heavily involved in the US business, especially in "promotions", Oldham encouraged the rumour and myth building around Klein - whose casual, pump-heeled approach disguised a ferocious business diligence. A meaty, dark-haired immigrant New Yorker in his early 30s, Klein kept it brief when he told the press: "Andrew manages the Rolling Stones and I manage him."

Oldham, 22, reflected on Klein's impact upon his life at the time: "I was an angry young man years ago simply because I hadn't got any money. Now, I suppose, I'm very nearly one of the people I hated so much. You grow up fast in this business or you get left behind. I know how to handle things artistically and creatively but Allen Klein knows how to convert my ideas into cash. Without his business brain I would go nowhere — just a bum with good ideas that would keep misfiring. I have no brain for money. I've been very cold for the past few weeks. Quite worrying, I've had the attitude that I'm the biggest con of all time. And I'm finding it more and more difficult to find a common ground between what I know is commercial and what offends my personal taste.

"When you get to this stage, you've got to be careful. You end up either a genius that's broke or a parasite that's a millionaire. It was as much luck as anything to get to the top. I had to learn the hard way and pass through a lot of phases — like aping Phil Spector[42]. You get bitten but you

---

42. Harvey Phillip Spector (1939–2021) was an American record producer and songwriter, best known for his innovative recording practices developing the Wall of Sound. Born in the Bronx, he moved to LA in 1958 as a founding member of the Teddy Bears, for whom he penned 'To Know Him Is to Love Him', a U.S. No. 1. In 1960 Spector co-founded Philles Records. By the age of 21 he was the youngest U.S. label owner and dubbed the "First Tycoon of Teen".

must experience it to know where you're going. You also have to have a fantastic ego and you go through a stage of thinking you're more important than the artists. I went through this with the Rolling Stones, but I'm sorted now. All you have to do when you arrive is make sure you don't go over the top. I'm working on that now. Yes, I'm rich and so are the Stones. Put it this way: we need never work again. But we couldn't pack it in. I suppose we all have big egos and we enjoy the fame and success of it all so much. Mick is the focal point and we all know it. The Rolling Stones can easily reach the Cliff Richard stage of carrying a lot of fans with them as years go by."

In this interview, Oldham once again brings to the fore his manic-depressive character, his self-doubt laid bare. Suffering from depression, in an earlier 'black mood' as it was called in 1963, after only six months of success with the Stones, Oldham had announced he was quitting show business, only to reconsider a week later: both pronouncements well-publicised by the press. Now he cut another Mick and Keith monster; '19th Nervous Breakdown'. It was harder and harsher than anything Oldham had produced with the group before; dense and malevolent, a storm brewing on Charlie's massive cymbal crashes and Keith's over-amped flourishes. As ugly as it was, it was another UK No. 1 in February '66

"The Stones are still social outcasts," Oldham reminded the press, in more familiar, expansive mood. "We work on the principle that if you are going to kick conformity in the teeth, you may as well use both feet."

The single, the group's sixth consecutive UK No. 1, went to No.2 in the US. It was followed by *Aftermath*, recorded entirely in LA which featured Stones versions of 'Think' and 'Out Of Time'. The album also went straight to No. 1 in the UK charts staying there for two months. In the US a "hits" album package *Big Hits (High Tide And Green Grass)* went to No.2. The Stones had, as Pete Townshend told me, "built a huge fucking wall between one generation and the next".

Who Are You?

Oldham was teenage pals with The Who's original manager Peter 'the Ace Face' Meaden who was two years his senior. Together they cut up Hampstead, Soho and the King's Road. The group's new managers, Kit Lambert and Chris Stamp, had removed the over-amped, pilled-out Meaden (Meaden had renamed the group The High Numbers, dressed them and written their songs) but had kept many of his Mod ideas to make the band famous. Lambert and Stamp were film-makers primarily and leaned on Oldham for music biz moves.

Oldham arranged — by phone from the back of the Phantom — for an incredulous Pete Townshend to fly over to New York to meet Allen Klein on a yacht on the Hudson River to discuss The Who's future. It was hot gossip in the music business that Lambert and Stamp had, in Stamp's words, "fucked up" with the deal they allowed The Who's producer, Shel Talmy, to make for the group's recordings. Talmy had signed the group to Decca US (a separate entity to Decca UK) and The Who's singles came out via Brunswick in the UK.

Rumours circulated that The Who were signing to Immediate and Townshend gave the label a song, 'Circles'. Tony Calder made a rare appearance in the studio with Jimmy Page to produce a version with Les Fleur de Lys. Page laid down a fuzz guitar lead line on the distinctive Whoesque track that lyrically spoke of typical Townshend teenage confusion.

"Peter Townshend is another who fascinates me," Oldham teased in the press. "He represents total escapism to the fans." Many such rumours swirled around Immediate:

they were linked to The Warriors[43], The Birds[44], and a 'tribute' album to Jim Reeves[45], with various Immediate acts recording one of his songs: a project, if it had been realised, that would have set the precedent for the now all-too-common tribute albums.

The Who rumour had legs: Klein tossed about the idea of Oldham coming on board with The Who as executive producer. Eventually Townshend stuck with Lambert and Stamp, who soon rectified the group's relationship with producer Talmy by getting rid of him. There was no small amount of fall-out back in London about this, in particular Klein's brusque attempt to land The Who.

Back on *terra firma* The Poets received more warm applause for a Gary Glitter/Andesound (another Oldham pseudonym) production and the ultimate Mod version — despite also being cut by The Who and the Small Faces — of the Holland/Dozier/Holland's 'Baby Don't Do It'. The Poets time at Immediate was all but over. They felt they were being short-changed by Tony Calder who preferred

---

43. The Warriors were a British beat band who recorded a few singles with Decca but are mostly remembered because many of its members (most notably Jon Anderson, who later fronted prog rock diehards Yes) later became successful musicians in the British progressive rock scene of the 1970s.

44. An English R&B band formed in 1964 in London notable for their guitarist, future Stones and Faces stalwart Ronnie Wood. When the US band The Byrds arrived in England for their first British tour in 1965 (with their single 'Mr Tambourine Man' high in the charts) Birds' manager Leo de Clerck took legal action to prevent them from using the name; the action failed, amid a flurry of national press and television coverage. The group parted ways with de Clerck soon afterwards.

45. James Travis Reeves (August 20, 1923 – July 31, 1964) was an American country singer and songwriter famous for songs such as 'Welcome to My World' and 'He'll Have To Go'. Reeves died on board the plane he was piloting when he got disorientated in a thunder storm.

to promote other Immediate acts such as London Waits (their baroque instrumental version of the theme tune to BBC1 programme, *Softly Softly*) and another flash-in-the-pan creation featuring Ron Wood of The Birds, on a Shel Talmy-produced track called 'Creation'.

Oldham believed another new signing to Immediate, New York's Goldie, fresh from leaving her backing group The Gingerbreads[46], had potential. He produced her singing a version of the aching Goffin/King number 'Goin' Back'. Unfortunately, Dusty Springfield released the same song and she ruled the roost after her recent No. 1, 'You Don't Have To Say You Love Me'. Goldie wasn't interested in duetting with Chris Farlowe and left Immediate three months later to record for Chris Blackwell at Island Records. In the 1970s she produced the first Dead Boys albums.

Incredibly, Oldham found time to make his fourth and final solo album, *The Rolling Stones Songbook*, one he considered his bible, "with the Stones as disciples and the songs as testaments". Oldham made Immediate promote his angel-voiced chorused and over-blown orchestrated versions of Jagger/Richards songs – 'The Last Time' (the version that provided the string riff for The Verve's 'Bitter Sweet Symphony'), 'Blue Turns To Grey', '(I Can't Get No) Satisfaction', 'Heart Of Stone', 'Tell Me', 'Congratulations', 'Play With Fire', and two he had helped them write, 'As Tears Go By' and 'Theme For A Rolling Stone' (both collaborative Oldham/Jagger/Richards tracks).

"A fantastic new album containing a dozen Rolling Stones numbers presented in subtle orchestral arrangements," ran the advert. "The idea is to prove that the Stones' music is not just a noise, but the melodies and idiom can stand up in any form," Oldham told the press.

---

46. Goldie & the Gingerbreads were the first all-female rock band signed to a major record label and toured the UK with the Stones and The Animals in 1964.

The Rolling Stones Songbook was released by Decca but working another label's records was nothing new at 138/147 Ivor Court. Oldham's best friend in LA, Lou Adler, manager of Johnny Rivers[47] and The Mamas & the Papas, had recently been the beneficiary of the treatment. Adler who lived in Bel Air, on Stone Canyon Road, and was the owner of Sunset Strip's most happening clubs, Whisky A-Go-Go, the Roxy and Rainbow, and co-writer, with Herb Alpert (who went on to form A&M records) and Sam Cooke of 'Wonderful World'.

Immediate staff were told to prioritise the new Mamas & the Papas UK single, 'California Dreamin'', even though it was coming out on EMI in the UK. In support of the song Oldham placed another full-page ad in the music press.

California Dreamin' by The Mamas and Papas

is more relative today

than the general election

which can only bring more bigotry,

unfulfilled promises

and the ultimate big bringdown.

'California Dreamin'' won't put the country

back on its feet

but it will give you a helluva lift

for two minutes and thirty-two seconds

and sometimes that can be a long time.

Andrew Loog Oldham, a bystander

p.s., I didn't write it, John Phillips did; I don't publish it,

47. Johnny Rivers (born John Henry Ramistella (1942-) is an American musician renowned for pop, folk, blues, and old-time rock 'n' roll. Rivers sang on a string of hit singles between 1964 and 1968, among them 'Memphis' (a Chuck Berry cover), and 'Baby I Need Your Lovin'' (a 1967 cover of the 1964 Four Tops single.

Trousdale do; I didn't produce it, Lou Adler did; and I don't release it, RCA do — I just like it...

Lou Adler: "I remember when the Mamas & the Papas first went to the UK, they went over on a boat. Why? There was no way of figuring out the reasons for their actions. Going on a boat could have been destructive or perhaps John reckoned they could rehearse on the way over. I went with Andrew to meet them and [Mama] Cass was arrested for stealing a blanket she had taken off the boat and the police took her to a local jail. It was great publicity. Andrew helped break the Mamas & the Papas in the UK; he definitely did, without a doubt. I'm sure the advert was just part of it. He never discussed it, never called and said, 'Look I would like to take an advert or I'm thinking about it'. You would just open up the paper up and there it was. He was laying the foundation for us."

Mother Cynthia

The success of the Stones was at its zenith, Immediate was the most happening record label in London, and Oldham was well into the throes of a full-on drug and drink addiction with marijuana, vodka, amphetamines and sleepers on heavy rotation. As a result the Ivor Court offices often threatened to spiral out of control, as staff freely indulged in following their leader's example.

Oldham recognised this and appointed himself a new personal assistant, Cynthia Gainsford, who was engaged to 'sixth' Stone Ian Stewart (who had been sacked by Oldham from the original Stones line-up for not looking the part). Cynthia had previously worked for Radio 1 DJ Alan Freeman and admired Oldham's style as he added an Aston Martin and grey Lotus to his fleet of cars. Under Gainsford, Oldham left behind his main style of long leather coats, silk Thea Porter Cossack blouses and hexagonal sunglasses and adopted a ferocious boardroom look in Roland Melandari suits, smartly clipped hair, bandit moustache and glasses with clear lenses to put on when reading contracts.

Cynthia Gainsford: "My value was social. I was never a secretary or anything like that. I couldn't type or do shorthand but I had very good contacts in the business and he needed somebody to block the public out. He started drinking; he had this globe you would open, full of vodka and Kalhúa, which made Black Russians. For a while he absolutely adored Black Russians, part of my job was to pour drinks and things. 138 Ivor Court was much more showbizzy than Calder's 147 office. Really Andrew was an owl, he would come in lateish in the mornings sometimes and work until late. After I married Stew, Andrew would say things like, 'Oh darling you can't go home', even though it was nine o'clock at night. I was always sort of watching over Andrew in a way."

"Before Cynthia arrived at Ivor Court it was fun," Tony King told me. "Then Cynthia organised everything, kept everything in order. I think he [Oldham] rather liked the idea of having a high-powered female personal assistant, she was quite ferocious and kept all sorts of people out of the office."

Dubbed the "Cassius Clay of record makers" in the press, Oldham was also now getting speed injections from Harley Street's infamous Doctor Robertson and in fact his new boardroom look was in large part down to an attempt to disguise his frequent and worryingly uncontrollable highs and lows. On top of all this Allen Klein had arranged another mammoth Stones tour of the US for late 66 — the last with the original line-up — covering 29 cities in 27 days.

That summer, in Hollywood at RCA studios on Sunset Strip, Oldham recorded a new Stones single, 'Paint It Black'. LA was boiling over, with riots happening right on the RCA studios' doorstep. A far cry from the previous year's Watts riots but nonetheless headline news. These riots were sparked by hundreds of kids congregating on the Strip, around Adler's clubs, expecting to party and causing traffic problems. Permits and licenses for clubs were withdrawn and a 10pm curfew for anyone under 18 was zealously enforced. There were protests and then riots. "Long Hair Nightmare" screamed the *LA Times*. One of the few winners appeared to be Buffalo Springfield, whose song, 'For What It's Worth', became an anthem for the city's youth movement.

'Paint It Black' blew everyone away, even The Beatles, and guaranteed a seventh consecutive UK No. 1 on advance orders of 300,000. According to Oldham it was "completely different from anything the boys have done as a single before". It was also a huge No. 1 in the US where its brooding sense of dark neurosis sent crowds crazy on the US tour; riots in some cities were so intense that Oldham and the band were often lucky to escape with their lives; buried under a five deep stage invasion when one venue's stage collapsed.

Afterwards the group were allowed their first proper break in three years - Jagger flew to Mexico, Richards stayed in New York, Bill Wyman and his wife went off to Florida, Charlie Watts to the Greek islands and Brian Jones to Tangiers with Anita Pallenberg.

Yet there was no rest for Oldham as he charged into a new era at Immediate, leaving behind the Ivor Court apartments and moving the whole outfit to a new address

Immediate House

If it had been all about "we're gonna get money" at Ivor Court, on New Oxford Street it was all about, "we've got money and now we're gonna spend it!" Immediate celebrated their first anniversary by making a documentary about themselves narrated by top Radio 1 DJ Alan Freeman, called *The Little Bastard Immediate*. The film was photographed, edited and directed by celebrated filmmaker Peter Whitehead. The idea was to use the 20-minute film to pump up the Philips sales and promotions forces around the UK and Europe. It opened with a naked women spread out on a table having her breasts painted to the sound of an exhilarating violin-led version of 'Paint It Black' sung by Chris Farlowe. It also featured Mick Jagger thanking everybody for helping promote 'Out Of Time' and promising he would be back in the country to produce Farlowe's next hit single.

Oldham had interior designer Robin Guild refurbish the new multi-roomed Immediate HQ, with separate elaborate main offices for himself and Calder, a music room and various other offices and alcoves for a growing workforce. Oldham had once hustled Guild in his weird and wacky Hampstead furniture store, keen at 17 to do PR for him. Then, when Guild got a bigger store in Hampstead, Oldham bought a chair from him for his mother. It turned out the chair would need a crane to get it in the flat and the deal ended up leaving the designer out of pocket.

Robin Guild: "Oldham said, 'I know exactly what I want, I want a place where I don't know where I am. I don't want to know what time of day it is and I want to be able to walk in wearing a Cecil Beaton hat or a Tibetan robe'. Tony Calder looks at me with his eyes up in the air. They had taken the first floor on a building on New Oxford Street: it was a building called Armward House. I noticed on the letterhead he had got Immediate Records, Immediate House, 63–69 New Oxford Street. I said, 'It's not Immediate House, it's Armward House'. Oldham said, 'Oh, I'm changing it'.

"One weekend he takes the name off the front of the building and calls it Immediate House, so when everybody comes to work on Monday all the addresses are wrong! He said, 'Oh they'll sue me but by the time they sue me I'll be long gone'.

"Tony Calder's office was done very modern for the period — a rosewood and black leather number. Andrew's office door looked like a cupboard from the outside. You opened these orange lacquer doors with big gold handles and stepped onto a marble platform, swung around 45 degrees and then you had to walk down three steps into Andrew's office. He sat himself at a table designed by the Finnish modernist Eero Saarinen[48], it had a tulip base with a white marble top; famous at the time. It was all very avant-garde for its day. It was photographed by *Ideal Home* magazine.

"It took quite a while to get the job done. The first scheme for Andrew's office, designed by his close friend Sean Kenny (the celebrated West End and Broadway theatre stage designer who worked closely with Lionel Bart on musicals such as *Oliver!*) was even weirder. You went through this cupboard into a circular Perspex chamber, like a revolving door, with spiral lines on the inside and outside. In the chamber the floor was gonna look like an album and

---

48. Eero Saarinen (1910-1961) was a Finnish-American architect and industrial designer who created a wide array of innovative designs for buildings and monuments, including Dulles International Airport in Washington, D.C., the TWA Flight Center (now TWA Hotel) at John F. Kennedy International Airport, and the Gateway Arch in St. Louis.

it would move so you felt as if you were going up, because of the way the spirals were working against each other. You felt like you were going up but in fact you were staying still. All it did was turn you around 45 degrees to face the right direction, to walk into Andrew's office.

"Inside Andrew's office you were facing the apex of a triangle. We were going to do it like a church. We were going to put in a pulpit, which was going to be Andrew's sort of desk, and the aisle was going to be mauve carpet that was made slightly narrower as it went away from you so that it made you feel the room was longer than it was. There were also bits of altar rail and choir stalls involved. The idea was that you had gone to heaven to meet Andrew Oldham. Andrew Oldham as God! He loved all this. There was going to be a huge crucifix behind his desk. But at the time there was The Beatles religious clash when Lennon said The Beatles were bigger than God and Andrew said, 'We can't do it now'.

"Andrew asked me, 'Do you do the inside of cars? I know exactly what I want: the car is black. It's got black windows, standard. We take the back seat out, so now we've got the boot as part of the interior. You put two-winged sort of club chairs back to the driver's bit and where the boot is you put a fireplace. In the fireplace we have one of those kitsch coal affect fires, with fans running to make shadows. Over the fireplace we have a picture frame, one of those baroque Golders Green, Jewish, gilt picture frames but no picture in it, just a white canvas. In the driver's compartment we put a projector and we project movies on the white canvas. Imagine I'm going up the M1, I'm facing the wrong way, the windows are dark, I don't know where I am, and I'm sat round the fireplace looking at the movies. What movies do I run? I run movies of road accidents, so it won't happen to me!'

"He always had this briefcase with him and alarms used to go off occasionally reminding him to take one concoction of pills or another, he used to carry a Luger in the briefcase as well. I remember once in New Oxford Street someone called up to say, 'There's a copper downstairs wants to see Andrew'. Oldham said to Calder, 'Oh you deal with it'. I said, 'You can't bring him in here, the place stinks of marijuana'. He said, 'They don't know anything' and disappeared through the communicating door between his and Calder's office. Calder is sitting there with his feet on the desk and this uniformed cop comes in, holding his helmet, a young cop looking pretty bewildered. The office is pretty palatial and all these sort of strange characters are wandering around. Calder says, 'Yes?' The copper says, 'Are you the owner of the vehicle....' Calder says, 'No'. The communicating door opens and Andrew leaps into the room Nureyev-style and shouts, 'I AM ANDREW OLDHAM!' he then proceeds to make this cop really wish he had never come into the office, giving him such a run around."

Immediate and Stones' record designer Steven Inglis recalled joining Immediate at the new offices: "I had this new wonderful office, a great big art table. Andrew more than tripled my *Ready Steady Go!* salary when I went to work full-time at Immediate as a designer. It was £10 a week from Immediate and £10 a week from the Stones. I redesigned *Aftermath* for America, and I did the cover of *Got Live If You Want It* for the Stones. On a design level Andrew would just sit and share his ideas and out of it something would emerge and we would use it.

"Then, come three o'clock in the afternoon, chauffeur Eddie would come and join me and mass-produce joints for Andrew. He would roll 20 or 30 joints and pack them up in cigarette packets and that's what Andrew would go out with for the evening. When you bought a custom Rolls Royce it wasn't uncommon for them to build in a jewel box, a little safe within the car where the lady was supposed to put her gems. Andrew had one of those in his Phantom 5 but it was full of drugs.

"The windows of the Rolls were all tinted black, except the driver's windows which were tinted green; it was illegal for the driver to have black windows back then. Andrew would drive along in the Rolls and cops would often stop them, just because they were curious to know who was in the car. Eddie was so fed up of being stopped for this reason that he used to have all his documents ready, he would just wind down his window about half an inch and poke [them] out. As the cops would walk towards the car, the centre divide would go up, sealing off the back, so Andrew was in his little cabin back there smoking a joint looking through the tinted glass at the cops looking at Eddie. In those days they could send you to jail for 15 years for marijuana.

"Cynthia was like Andrew's Margaret Thatcher — the office mother. The relationship between Andrew and Tony Calder was like a Jekyll and Hyde partnership. Andrew's up there, everybody loves Andrew, we're following Andrew; meanwhile Tony Calder's telling us to sign this and sign that. Sean Kenny was often around; he would keep Andrew's creative juices flowing.

"Artists started signing to Immediate because Andrew had done it with the Stones. Gered Mankowitz was doing all our photography — the Stones and Immediate. Mankowitz lived in Fulham just across the road from Broadway station. We used to ride into the office together in the morning and stop off at Fortnum and Mason's to have breakfast... we were always working together during the day on different projects at Immediate."

Gered Mankowitz, the Stones' official photographer: "Everybody loved my pictures of Marianne [Faithfull] and Andrew Oldham and Tony Calder asked if I would like to photograph the Stones. I replaced [David] Bailey. Andrew was open to me because he liked the fact that my father was a screenwriter in show business, especially as he had written *Expresso Bongo*. I have an image of Immediate, 1966–68, as being just a glorious time of fantastic creativity. Just mad, fun, extremely creative, a feeling of being very much on top of the tree, top of the pile, the music and energy was fantastic. We were having so much fun. Andrew was just the most fantastic person to be with, we went out quite a lot; he had the cars and the big house.

"I was with Immediate most of the time, spending a lot of evenings taking photographs, coming up with ideas, doing designs, adverts, sales presentations, hanging with Andrew, going to recording studios, radio stations, y'know, looning, having a great time. Andrew coaxed performances out of people in the studio, he would say I don't think that's working, try it with a bit more... he used funny language and body movements to communicate in the studio. It was like he was directing traffic.

"Immediate was the *enfant terrible* of the record business; we were having hits, making great music. A lot of planning and manipulation went into it — this wasn't accidental. Andrew loved Immediate, he loved the way of life, and he loved being the slightly villainous head of a record company, the whole operation. He used to have a fantastic wardrobe of clothes, all arranged by colour, jackets and suits, start with white and end up in black – just an immaculate guy right?"

Future General Manager of Immediate, Paul Banes, joined the company at New Oxford Street, starting out as assistant to Immediate and Stones' accountant Stan Blackbourne: "At the UK office you came into Immediate and on the right hand side you had the reception, on the left there was a little corridor going back. At the end of the corridor was a music room, where we put all our gear and did demos on a Revox. The first office on the left was mine and Stan's office, it was next door to Ken Mewis [the new promotions manager] who had an assistant, called Pauline, who went to RCA after Immediate. We had a girl on reception, very East Anglia, awfully, awfully posh girl. Then there was a big double door that went into what they

called New York and LA. New York was Tony's, on the
left. It had a wooden panelled office, big leather desk, big
leather sofas. Outside his office there was Jenny. Then in the
back, LA, Andrew's office, he had a big fashionable marble
topped table, white seats. Their two offices took up 95 per
cent of the space really.

"I was the third oldest when I started there and I was 20,"
Banes laughs, "Immediate were miles in front of everybody
else. The whole thing was streets ahead, the attitude, the
rapport we had with the artists. The Immediate staff were
tight and dedicated, we buckled down to do the work. When
a record went in at No. 1 we were all happy, and it just stuck
a couple of fingers up at the people down the road. That's
what it was all about!"

Oldham gave *NME* reporter Keith Altham a tour
of the new Immediate offices for a double-page spread
headed: "Oldham: Talented, Insulting, Outrageous".
Oldham was described as "agitated, bouncing about
among the packing cases" but had to leave for a flight to
New York in 15 minutes. Altham joined him and Calder
in the Phantom 5 on the way to the airport. "I'm going to
New York then chartering a private plane to Hollywood,"
Oldham told Altham. "Allen Klein and I are negotiating
an outlet for Immediate Records in the US and we also
have to discuss plans for the Stones film." He also gossiped
about Marianne Faithfull ("Nothing to do with me now"),
and the Stones girls, Chrissie Shrimpton, Linda Keith and
Anita Pallenberg.

The Rolls Royce stopped off at Oldham's Fulham
residence and then cruised on to the airport. From the back
seat, "with the push of a button", Oldham asked chauffeur
Eddie to drop off a torn suit at Lord Johns for "invisible
repair". Oldham told Altham he was moving home too —
from the Fulham house into a mansion in Highgate built by

Oliver Cromwell's brother[49]. As for Immediate, Oldham said he had plans for a big name signing but the details "were still being negotiated".

"There are lots of egos involved and it depends on something which depends on something else if you see what I mean," Oldham told Altham.

Then he talked up new signing Twice As Much. "I would say they have the same kind of mass appeal as Cliff Richard" — "worldwide" said Calder finishing his sentence. "Universal simplicity," trumped Oldham.

When asked about Nico — who was used in the photo to accompany the *NME* piece — Oldham said she was now working with The Velvet Underground, earning around £11,000 for eight days in clubs such as Hollywood Trip. Altham wrote how he was astonished to hear Oldham compare Scott Walker to Joan Crawford, and declare, "The new Beach Boys single is not dedicated to me".

However, Oldham was all business when discussing the Stones. Altham brought up a recent New York-based Stones show which he said attracted "only" 11,000 people. "Anyone would think it was bad," Oldham said. "The date was a weekend booking with temperatures in the nineties. It was the equivalent of playing in Piccadilly Garden on a bank holiday and 11,000 for that ain't bad."

Altham decided Oldham was "going in several directions at once — mostly up", concluding, "Andrew Oldham is egotistical, talented, insulting, outrageous, and likeable almost in spite of himself. He manages the world's number two group, owns his own record company, produces discs, writes songs, sleeve notes and poetry and publishes the Beach Boys music in Britain. In the hip

---

49. This was almost certainly a lie as Wikipedia states, "Robert Williams, alias Cromwell (c. 1560–1617), who married Elizabeth Steward (c. 1564–1654), probably in 1591, the couple had ten children, but Oliver, the fifth child, was the only boy to survive infancy."

vocabulary of pop music they say he is happening. Perhaps Mama Cass stressed what is the most overlooked and often unconsidered feature in Oldham's success when she incredulously repeated to me over and over again during a recent interview. 'And he's only 22 — can you imagine what he'll be doing when he's 30!'

Beach Boys

Immediate established a sister company, Immediate (London) Music, at New Oxford Street - the label's publishing arm and the start of a new empire. Oldham had cut a savvy publishing deal for Jagger/Richards songs with main London firm, Essex Music, way back in 1963. It had been a simple 50/50 deal but Oldham had got himself a sizeable share of the Jagger/Richards 50%. His cut on those songs still keeps him living in style today. And when publishers tried to push their own songwriters and songs on Oldham for possible use with the Stones or Immediate, he was always pushy back, angling to grab a slice of the publishing on the song for his own ends. Oldham had picked up tricks off Phil Spector too, notably his proclivity for writing the b-sides to hit singles, the publishing proceeds of which tended to be split equally between a and b side.

Now Oldham and Calder didn't want to cut deals with established publishers but to own the songs outright. They consulted Essex Music boss David Platz which led to Immediate releasing a real oddity in their catalogue, the *Who Can I Turn To?* album by Mark Murphy[50], a Sinatra-era jazz crooner who both Ella Fitzgerald and Scott Walker adored. Platz had paid for the recording of the Murphy

---

50. Mark Howe Murphy (1932–2015) was an American jazz singer based at various times in New York City, Los Angeles, London, and San Francisco. He recorded 51 albums under his own name during his lifetime and was principally known for his innovative vocal improvisations. He was the recipient of the 1996, 1997, 2000, and 2001 *Down Beat* magazine readers' jazz poll for Best Male Vocalist and was also nominated five times for the Grammy Award for Best Vocal Jazz Performance.

album. The singer was a star at Ronnie Scott's and landed his own BBC2 television show and sales were relatively brisk but it was done as a favour to Platz who would soon be boss of EMI's Regal Zonophone label, a reactivated old jazz imprint, intended as EMI's version of the "artistically free Immediate".

Alongside Essex Music, the other major music publishing company in London was Carlin Music, run by Oldham's pal, 'Viennese Freddie' Bienstock[51], who had grown hugely wealthy by owning the copyrights to an incredible catalogue of songs. Each time one of Carlin's songs was performed, played or covered — on the radio or stage — Freddie collected a small "performance rights" fee (one play on BBC radio at the time was worth about £2). Publishing revenues were routinely split 50/50 between the collecting publisher and the songwriter. Morris Levy's famous quote was: "The song works for itself and it never talks back to you." He added: "It is just pennies but it all accumulates to nice money."

Oldham and Calder began to sign specialist songwriters to provide songs for Immediate (London) Music and to encourage artists releasing records on Immediate to place their songs with their new publishing company, not Essex, Carlin or indeed Dick Rowe, who owned The Beatles song

---

51. Freddy Bienstock (1923–2009) began his career by soliciting and selecting songs for Elvis Presley's early albums and films. Bienstock would claim that "for the first 12 years of his career, Elvis wouldn't look at a song unless I'd seen it already." In the 1960s Bienstock required about ten original songs for each Elvis movie, with as many as four films produced annually. With so many songwriters anxious to get their songs published and performed by Presley, Bienstock was successful in demanding that a substantial portion of royalties that the writer would normally receive would be given to Presley and Hill & Range, a practice called "the Elvis Tax". Bienstock purchased Belinda Music, Hill & Range's subsidiary in the UK, in 1966 and changed its name to Carlin Music after his daughter, Caroline.

publishing and whose offices Immediate had moved into next door on New Oxford Street.

One of Immediate Music's first signings was Wayne Fontana, who had dropped the Mindbenders and penned the exquisite 'Game Of Love', a sure-fire earner but the buzz surrounding the new company was amplified with the press announcement that Immediate Music had secured the UK rights to the Beach Boys songs.

The group's records were released by EMI in the UK but they had not had a UK Top 10 entry for almost two years, since 'I Get Around' in 1964. Oldham was a big fan, as witnessed by the 1965 Andrew Loog Oldham Orchestra album, *East Meets West*, which featured one side of Beach Boys covers and one side of Four Seasons covers. The deal saw the songs of Brian Wilson used for a slew of new Immediate releases: The Factotums recorded the everlasting 'You're So Good To Me', as did Chris Farlowe and Twice As Much; 'Girl Don't Tell Me' was recorded by the Brian Epstein managed act Tony Rivers[52] and The Castaways while 'Barbara Ann' was recorded by The Masterminds.

When The Beach Boys twigged and released 'Barbara Ann' as a single in the UK it was the start of a majestic renaissance, five UK Top 5 singles followed in 1966, with songs such as 'Sloop John B', 'God Only Knows', 'Good Vibrations', 'Help Me Rhonda', 'Heroes and Villains' and 'California Girls' all earning and not talking back for Immediate Music.

Tony Calder: "EMI didn't want to know about The Beach Boys, they were just one of those surf bands from the West Coast. EMI didn't want to promote some band that

---

52. Tony Rivers, born Douglas Anthony Thompson, (1940-) is an English singer, best known for singing with the groups Tony Rivers and the Castaways and Harmony Grass. Rivers also sang on albums by Steve Harley & Cockney Rebel, Roger Daltrey, Shakin' Stevens and Cliff Richard and also performed many cover versions on the *Top of the Pops* records.

went surfing. Surf and sunshine? What did that mean in England? EMI didn't realise that Brian was a great talent. We broke them in this country. We were doing press on them, getting interviews for them, taking adverts. That's how we got the publishing — as a reward. I remember EMI rang us up and said, 'What have you done with this Beach Boys record?' I said, 'We've put it in the charts'. They said, 'Yeah, I can see that but we haven't even manufactured it yet'. I said, 'Well how long do you want?' They said, 'Well it'll be ready next week'. I said, 'Okay, I'll put it up a place'. So we paid the guy who fixed the charts at one of the music papers another hundred quid. The guy from EMI rang up and said, 'We've still got a problem'. I said, 'Okay, one more week'."

Immediate Music also released sheet music by blues legend, Robert Johnson[53], although their ownership of his catalogue may have been fleeting. The Beach Boys catalogue didn't stay with Immediate Music long either. Their manager, Murry Wilson, used Immediate's tardiness in making publishing payments and the success of the group's Immediate-fuelled UK hits to land his boys a big advance for the group's publishing. Before that Oldham bathed in an advance copy of the new Beach Boys album *Pet Sounds*, listening to it intently in hotel rooms from Manchester to Stockholm. He took out his own adverts in the music press to compare it to Rimsky-Korsakov's *Scheherazade* and then steadied himself to record an album that could compete.

---

53. Robert Leroy Johnson (1911–1938) was an American blues musician and songwriter whose landmark recordings in 1936 and 1937 displayed a combination of singing, guitar skills, and songwriting talent that has influenced later generations of musicians.

Sittin' on a Fence

Immediate had signed young, green, folky songwriters, Andrew Skinner and David Rose, after Oldham asked Cynthia to play him every tape that had been sent in to the Immediate office by aspiring acts over the past few months. Oldham spent days listening to a hundred tapes or more before choosing Rose and Skinner as winners and arranging for them to make a small budget demo of their songs. He dreamed up a name for them, Twice As Much, before handing them a Jagger/Richards song, 'Sittin' on a Fence' to record as their debut (while encouraging the duo to develop as songwriters).

"He would say, 'Here's two or three records, take a bit of that, take a bit out of this'," said Skinner. With Oldham producing, 'Sittin' on a Fence' was recorded at Pye studios with Art Greenslade and a full orchestra; the ornate Elizabethan, harpsichord-heavy backing giving it a quaint feel, before being mixed hard in New York. Apparently, Oldham had got the name Twice As Much from a *Time* magazine article he read on the flight back from the mixing, after toying with idea of launching them as David and Andrew.

Twice As Much were given a big push by Immediate, with adverts touting them as "The Hit Summer Sound of Young England". Oldham introduced them on the television show *Thank Your Lucky Stars*[54] and was quoted in

---

54. *Thank Your Lucky Stars* was a pop music show made by ABC Weekend TV, and broadcast on ITV 1961-66. Of all the show's presenters, Brian Matthew is perhaps the best remembered. Many of the leading pop groups of the time performed on it. As well as featuring British artists, it often included American guest stars.

the press saying: "Not since Marianne Faithfull have I gone
overboard like this on an act. They are tomorrow and new
when all other newness has subsided into yesterday. One
is good looking and the other is the sort that people think
looks like them. A certain part of the act must be a mirror
for the audience to see themselves in."

When 'Sittin' On A Fence' cracked the Top 20, peaking
at No.12, self-congratulatory Immediate adverts went
across the press, announcing the single's chart achievement
with a special mention for arranger Art Greenslade. Twice
As Much followed the hit with two more singles, both original
Skinner and Rose compositions. 'Step Out Of Line' peaking
at No.29 and 'True Story' which had Billy Fury proclaiming
in *Melody Maker*: "It's a great arrangement. I'll bet Andrew
Oldham had a hand in that."

Oldham produced both singles, skilfully managing the
orchestration, allowing the smooth harmonising from the
group and sophisticated song themes to shine. Oldham then
poured his money, blood, sweat and tears into recording the
debut Twice As Much album, his *Pet Sounds*. It was called *Own
Up*; a "grand, epic, symphonic, fantasy" production that cost
£26,000 to record (a then benchmark for the cost of making
an album) and took about three weeks to complete (the
industry standard for albums was three days in 1966).

Art Greenslade, arranger on *Own Up*: "The Twice As
Much album was inspired by *Pet Sounds*. It came out before
Sgt. Pepper's Lonely Hearts Club Band and I thought it was
better. Andrew had a lot of strange ideas, and a lot of them
came off. We spent a lot of time on that album; damn lot of
work went into it. We would finish a session, get the backing
track down and Andrew would sit there all night, just keep
listening to this backing track played back to him.

"He was a very thorough man, a very clever guy.
We would get in the studio and he would start kicking
it around. Once we had run through, he would start
changing things, if it were possible to be changed. We

had some very good, very clever sessions. Andrew used his favourite musicians. His favourite drummer was Andy White, who had done some sessions with The Beatles. Andrew would go down the stairs, go into the drum booth and spend five minutes just getting this little drum fill in, spend the time to get what he wanted, just this stupid little drum fill, you wouldn't bloody know, it wouldn't sell the record, if you blinked your eye it would be gone."

Own Up was recorded at PYE studios, where The Who, The Kinks and The Spencer Davis Group all recorded. Oldham booked the cream of session musicians for the project including Jimmy Page and Jim Sullivan and pianist/ keyboardist, Nicky Hopkins. John Paul Jones remembers playing bass along with a stand-up string bass and there was a double rhythm section, three percussionists, two drummers and a full orchestra.

The first woman of rock journalism and the London *Evening Standard*'s young culture writer, Maureen Cleave — she who had got the Jesus quote out of Lennon and was the first to interview Phil Spector in this country — went down to the studio as the album was being recorded for an Oldham profile. "Mr Oldham looks like an impatient world-weary, Little Lord Fauntleroy", Cleave teased. "There are golden curls about his ears and dark glasses just as permanently on his nose. He is tall and very skinny with his bell-bottomed jeans. He sometimes wears ruffled shirts and Tom Jones shoes with buckles. His appearance and manner madden many people. 'They think I'm a rude lout,' he says."

Cleave described the scene in the "dark recording studio": "Four young men sitting on the floor, two more singing 'ooh' into a microphone, another, his chauffeur, leaning against the door, a girl singing behind a screen and a teenage guitarist and pianist playing their heads off.

"Behind a wall of glass facing them Mr Oldham was soundlessly making the most extraordinary faces and gestures of encouragement to the girl. 'Bah, bah, bah,' he appeared to say as he jerked his head back and forth like a hen in time to the music. Occasionally his voice boomed forth, 'I want the ending nice like surf crashing against rocks', or 'I want it very haunting like monks in cassocks'."

"Beethoven goes Latin" or "very wankable, very wankable" might also have spilled out. When it came to a passage for saxophones, Oldham would assume his saxophone pose. There is a film recording of him in the studio producing *Own Up* as he sings Skinner and Rose through an opening line. Take after take is stopped, being not good enough, before Oldham sings it down to them from the control booth the way he wants it and then they nail it.

During the sessions for *Own Up* members of a large string ensemble were overheard in the toilet saying, "God this is bloody rubbish, when's it gonna be over". Oldham obtained all their names and booked them again on a really hot day, turned the air con off, and had nothing for them to play. He just sat in front of them for three hours.

David Skinner of Twice As Much: "*Own Up* was his baby, he put a lot of effort into it. He was meticulous with it, he used to go back to New York and remix things. It was incredibly meticulously made. I certainly didn't see any money out of it, nothing substantial, like you could say, well I earned so much out of that album; everything got absorbed by the living and the making of it."

Own Up featured lavish versions of The Beatles 'Help' and 'We Can Work It Out', Spector/Goffin/King's 'Is This What I Get For Loving You Baby', Jagger/Richards/Oldham's 'As Tears Go By' and a slowed down and symphonic version of the Small Faces' recent hit 'Sha La La La Lee', plus original contributions from Skinner and Rose, one, 'Life Is But Nothing', would be covered by many Immediate artists to come.

"The sound is absolutely fantastic," reckoned the *NME*

review, Skinner and Rose's harmonies sat atop "exquisitely layered rhythms with blasts of orchestral punctuations from trombones, chiming bells and tinkling harpsichords, cuckoo and raindrop effects". The review concluded: "Teenage angst, street corner doo-wop, this is an English symphonic look at the theme of love".

The album never quite got the same recognition as *Pet Sounds* or indeed *Sgt Pepper*, but the making of it — the gesture at least — awakened many musicians to the way it could be, with an eye on the art.

Small Faces' singer Steve Marriott brought it up in interviews at the time: "A record like this opens up somebody's mind and makes the way for another record even better. I really dig Andrew Oldham. He's too much. On a scene of his very own and it's great."

It was after reading these comments that Oldham had phoned Marriott: "He was interested in working with us; did we have any songs?"

The previous time someone had tried to steal Marriott and the Small Faces from their manager Don Arden, they had ended up being dangled by their ankles from a fourth-floor balcony[55]. Now, though, the nation's undisputed No 1 Mod outfit were giving Arden enough of a headache for him to take a more prosaic approach. The "ungrateful bastards" refused to play 'Sha La La La Lee' on any of their live dates, were bitching about their new single 'My Mind's Eye' and had just gotten themselves banned from *Top Of The Pops*.

A give-away something was afoot came with Chris Farlowe's new single, the Marriott/Lane song 'My Way Of Giving' which, despite being "produced by Mick Jagger",

---

55. Hearing that Australian entrepreneur Robert Stigwood (future manager of Cream and The Bee Gees) was interested in the band, Don and his heavies paid Stigwood a visit and dangled him off his fourth-floor balcony as a warning.

failed to make the Top 40. It was recorded at the same time as the Stones were making their next album *Between The Buttons* at London's Olympic studios. Farlowe remembered Marriott and fellow Small Face Ronnie Lane taking control in Olympic with assistance from various Stones. It was "a crazy session," Farlowe said.

Oldham was a pal of Arden's from way back. Don had the Small Faces on a deal with Decca Records via his own production company Contemporary and there was some talk of the group recording a Stones' song, while Twice as Much cut another Marriott/Lane track 'Green Circles'.

First Cut Is The Deepest

It was Mick Jagger who was first knocked out by 21-year-old Pat Arnold. The LA singer had been persuaded to quit her role as a hard-working Ikette in the Ike and Tina Turner Revue after their 1966 UK tour with the Stones and sign a solo deal with Immediate. Since then she'd stayed with the label's designer, Steven Inglis, and his girlfriend, in their London flat, working with various Immediate musicians in the studio and "waiting for the right track to come along". Gered Mankowitz had christened her PP, and the original plan had been for Jagger to write and produce her, replicating the process that had brought Chris Farlowe's success.

Instead, PP's Immediate debut was a version of 'Everything's Gonna Be Alright', co-written (with David Skinner) and produced by Oldham and arranged by Art Greenslade. Arnold told the press that Oldham had intended her to record 'Is This What I Get For Loving You' by Goffin/King/Spector, the only Ronnettes failure in their run of hits, but the song had been in the wrong key for her voice.

'Everything's Gonna Be Alright' backed by Twice As Much's 'Life Is But Nothing' sank so fast that many considered PP's Immediate follow-up, 'First Cut Is The Deepest' to be her debut. Years later, however, 'Everything's Gonna Be Alright' was repressed and became a Northern Soul favourite.

Arnold got lucky. One door from Immediate at New Oxford Street was the office of Beatles publisher Dick James, who — since his incredible stroke of fortune courtesy of Brian Epstein — had built a respectable publishing

company with a stable of young writers, among them Elton
John and Cat Stevens[56]. Stevens was breaking as a recording
artist in his own right with the album *Matthew and Son*,
the first release on Deram, Decca's new "contemporary"
Immediate-styled label.

The young, bearded songwriter was a familiar face
at Immediate as his father ran a sandwich bar below the
office. Stevens' managers, Mike Hurst (a former member of
The Springfields) and Chris Brough (son of 50's *Educating
Archie* ventriloquist Peter Brough), thought Arnold had
a lot of potential. Hurst, who had produced *Matthew and
Son*, was enthusiastic about producing her in the studio and
Immediate agreed he take her there with a new Stevens
song, 'First Cut Is The Deepest'.

With Greenslade laying on the orchestration and
Arnold giving it the full on treatment as per her former lead,
Tina Turner, the strength of the song was undeniable and
Arnold was nothing if not a hard worker and she pushed
'First Cut Is The Deepest' with incredible determination
and drive. The single went into the Top 20 in the UK
and broke across Europe. Arnold performed live and on
television in Germany, Switzerland, Greece and Belgium
and raved about her Immediate backing group on these
dates, "a little four-piece band called The Nice". Arnold
was "hoping to add a trumpet and tenor sax" to the band
for her own soul revue.

---

56. The son of a Cypriot restaurateur, Stevens was born Steven
Demetre Georgiou (1948-) and recorded a string of hit albums in the
late 60s/early 70s: *Matthew and Son* (1967) reached top ten in the UK
charts. Stevens' albums *Tea for the Tillerman* (1970) and *Teaser and the
Firecat* (1971) were certified triple platinum in the US and *Catch Bull at
Four* (1972) went to No.1 on the Billboard 200.

Stevens converted to Islam in December 1977 and adopted the
name Yusuf Islam the following year. In 1979 he auctioned all of his
guitars for charity and left his musical career to devote himself to
educational and philanthropic causes in the Muslim community.

On the back of the success of 'First Cut Is The Deepest', Mike Hurst produced a run of Oldham-lite minor singles for Immediate: 'Black Sheep RIP' by The Australian Playboys[57] (the nursery rhyme 'Baa Baa Black Sheep' set to music), 'She Was Perfection' by actor/singer/songwriter Murray Head[58], 'Sticks and Stones' by Warm Sounds[59], the single 'Moanin'' with Chris Farlowe, and PP's third single, 'The Time Has Come', by one of his own writers, Paul Korda, which peaked in the UK at No.35.

Chris Farlowe went back to formula with a fantastic Art Greenslade orchestrated, Mick Jagger produced, version of 'Yesterday's Papers', a fresh Jagger/Richards track off the new Stones' album in the making, *Between The Buttons*. Immediate's use of Jagger/Richards tracks ahead of the band were often their most creative and commercially successful (for the Stones at least) releases. The radically re-recorded songs would often be given fresh depth by dramatic string motifs. Moody-looking Immediate newcomer, Nicky Scott, managed by Yardbird manager Simon Napier-Bell[60], covered another Jagger/Richards track from *Between The Buttons*; 'Backstreet Girl'. With Jagger on backing vocals, the

---

57. The Australian Playboys was the name given to the Melbourne-spawned rock & roll band The Playboys, for their appearances and record releases outside of Australia, to avoid confusion with Gary Lewis's backing band "the Playboys."

58. Murray Seafield St George Head (1946-) is an English actor and singer who appeared in a number of films, including a starring role as the character Bob Elkin in the Oscar-nominated 1971 film *Sunday Bloody Sunday*. As a musician, he is most recognised for his international hit songs 'Superstar' (from *Jesus Christ Superstar*) and 'One Night in Bangkok'.

59. Warm Sounds were an English musical duo, consisting of Denver Gerrard and Barry Younghusband, and later adding John Carr. They are considered a one hit wonder for their 1967 hit single, 'Birds and Bees'.

60. Simon Robert Napier-Bell (1939-) managed artists as diverse as the Yardbirds, Marc Bolan, Boney M, Wham! and Candi Staton.

Scott single was publicised as being produced by Jagger and Oldham, but Jagger's reluctance to help out on promotion in any real terms hindered Scott's chances. A change of tack for his second Immediate single, a limp Oldham-produced version of 'Big City', did equally poorly and Scott was dropped from the label.

The chart misses piled up but the fun never stopped. 'The Changing Of The Guard' by The Marquis of Kensington was a front for Kinks manager Robert Wace, whose identity on the track was a poorly-kept secret. Wace had originally hired The Kinks to back him at a party, only to come off stage and decide, along with his friend Grenville Collins to manage the "backing band". The single is strong evidence of his influence on Ray Davies' songwriting and the b-side is likely to have featured The Kinks themselves.

Via Lou Adler, Immediate picked up 'You Baby' by The Turtles, a US Top 20, for UK release. It was written by PF Sloan and Steve Barri, who had also penned the Barry McGuire hit 'Eve Of Destruction' for Adler's independent label Dunhill. Oldham had been a huge fan of The Turtles[61] previous smash, 'Happy Together'.

Art Greenslade arranged a catchy, upbeat, new Twice As Much single, 'Crystal Ball', which also happened to be the name of a prostitute Oldham had invited up the offices with a view to recording. The song was written by Kenny Lynch[62] and US songwriter Mort Shuman who, with his

---

61. The Turtles are an LA rock band formed in 1965, best known for the 1967 hit song 'Happy Together'. They charted several other top 40 hits, including 'It Ain't Me Babe' (1965), 'You Baby' (1966) and 'She'd Rather Be With Me' (1967).
62. Kenneth Lynch, OBE (1938–2019) was an English singer, songwriter, entertainer, and actor and one of the few black singers in British pop music. Whilst on tour with The Beatles, Lynch reportedly offered to help them write a song, but quickly became frustrated and criticised their ability to compose music – at the time Lennon and McCartney were writing 'From Me to You'.

original songwriting partner Doc Pomus, had written classics such as 'Teenager In Love', 'Can't Get Used To Losing You' and 'Save The Last Dance For Me'. Shuman had also co-written, with Lynch, 'Sha La La La Lee' for the Small Faces.

Oldham took Shuman into the studio to record an instrumental version of the Mamas & the Papas hit 'Monday Monday' for Immediate. The songwriter left a more lasting impression by introducing the music of Jacques Brel to Oldham at the Immediate offices. Shuman was an *oficiado*: he would go on to handle the English translations of Brel and produce an off-Broadway musical smash *Jacques Brel Is Alive And Well And Living in Paris* that made Shuman a star in 1970s and 80s France.

Oldham left London with Shuman, flying to New York to record with one of Allen Klein's clients, Bobby Vinton, (the successful hit balladeer, best remembered for 'Blue Velvet'). At CBS studios, with Shuman arranging, Vinton attempted to sing his way through Oldham's symphonic Beach Boys 'Good Vibrations'-style production of *West Side Story*'s, 'I Have A Love'. The track was completely unsuitable for Vinton and was never released. Shuman remembered he and Oldham being "Black Russianed to oblivion".

In New York, Oldham ended Immediate's relationship with Bert Berns' record label Bang! Berns[63] and his label had started the whole ball rolling with 'Hang On Sloopy' but subsequent McCoys singles had failed to sell. The

---

63. Bertrand Russell Berns (1929–1967), also known as Bert Russell and (occasionally) Russell Byrd, was an American songwriter and record producer of the 1960s. His songwriting credits include 'Twist and Shout', 'Piece of My Heart', 'Here Comes the Night', 'Hang on Sloopy', 'Cry to Me' and 'Everybody Needs Somebody to Love'. Berns, who had a history of cardiac trouble as a result of his heart being damaged from rheumatic fever contracted during childhood, died in his New York apartment of heart failure on December 30, 1967, aged 38.

group, largely the construct of a back-room production team, had enjoyed a run of Top 20 singles in the US, all issued to little success in the UK by Immediate. A full-page music advert commemorated the amicable split.

A lot of these mid-to-late 1966 Immediate releases (with rare exceptions) do not stand up to further listening. It was obvious to Immediate that in Arnold they had a great voice, but supplying her with the right material was still hit and miss. Farlowe's take on the Stones tracks was well-executed but seemed inadequate if you could have the original, and Twice As Much lacked oomph. As for the rest of the releases, novelty were their only redeeming feature. The label needed some grounding before it floated off on a cloud of marijuana smoke.

Small Faces

After 'Whatcha Gonna Do About It', 'Sha La La La Lee' and 'All Or Nothing', the Small Faces were closing 1966 in the UK Top 5 with their latest single, 'My Mind's Eye'. They were the nation's No 1 Mod group, having been discovered, managed, produced and promoted to stardom by the infamous Don Arden[64]. "In those days I had the power to phone up anyone in the business, through being Europe's No. 1 concert promoter," he told me, "I phoned up *Top of the Pops* and bosh! The Small Faces were on the show."

Arden remains an anathema to the modern British music business, and yet he is a giant and a great: the most influential British rock 'n' roll promoter of all time, responsible for bringing over the first wave of US rock to the UK in the late 1950s, early 60s: Sam Cooke, Jerry Lee Lewis, Little Richard, Bo Diddley, Chuck Berry, Ray Charles, Fats Domino, The Everly Brothers and many, many more. He had moved on to developing UK pop acts after The Beatles destroyed these idols and ticket sales for his stable "died a death overnight".

Arden: "The Small Faces was the first time that I really

---

64. Born into a poor and ghettoised Jewish family in Cheetham Hill, Manchester, Don Arden [1926-2007] (real name Harry Levy) began his show business career when he was just 13 years old as a singer and stand-up comic. After being demobilised from the British Army at the end of the war, he began a career as concert promoter and manager – combining both when he brought over Gene Vincent for a series of shows in 1960. Music biz legend has it in 1964 he signed up the Small Faces on the spot and paid £12,000 to fix the charts for their first single to be a hit and the rest is music legend.

got stuck in. I found them, recorded them, released their first single and got them in the Top 10 in six weeks. That's all it took, six weeks! I had 'Whatcha Gonna Do About It' on my shelf; a couple of the guys that worked for me for £25 a week, Brian Potter and Ian 'Sammy' Samwell wrote the song. After the first smash hit the Small Faces said they didn't wanna work with Sammy anymore because they were ungrateful bastards. He cried his fucking eyes out and there was nothing I could do about it.

Arden: "I offered the Small Faces to Immediate when they first started. Stevie [Marriott] knew Tony Calder, but he never did anything for them. Andrew didn't see the commerciality in them. he turned them down, and he didn't want to know. To me the Faces had an image of their own; they looked like four little Oliver Twists — street urchins. When they came out they looked like four half-grown kids, and when they opened up the sound was so powerful — that was the impact. That's the way it hit me the first time I saw them, I thought, 'They can't fail'."

Now Arden had a new act, Amen Corner, and the £25,000 Immediate were offering for the Small Faces was some pay-off.

Don Arden: "It's a funny thing how people like Calder talk: 'Oh yes I bought the Small Faces from Don Arden'. Tony Calder is full of shit. First of all if he ever bought anything, it was on behalf of Immediate, if he ever did anything it was on behalf of Oldham really. He was a bullshitter, all the time. I never liked him and I never trusted him. I sold the Small Faces recording contract to Harold Davison[65] [Frank's Sinatra's UK agent/impresario] then he sold it on to Immediate. Calder saying, 'Oh yeah, we bought

---

65. Harold Davison (1922-2011) was a producer known for *BBC Show of the Week* (1965), *Frank Sinatra: In Concert at the Royal Festival Hall* (1970) and *Night of Nights* (1970). He is also credited for being the first to book Frank Sinatra and Judy Garland to concerts in the UK and taking the Stones to the US.

the record contract for £25,000 from Don, delivered it to him in a brown paper bag because he needed the cash at the time'. Calder would always put something like that in to try and bring me down. I always hated Calder and he hated me. We hated each other."

Oldham recollects Allen Klein wiring him the money for the Small Faces, putting £25,000 in a brown paper bag and giving it to Arden, who was then happy to induce a breach of contract with Decca, allowing the Small Faces to sign with Immediate. The money was a colossal amount to pay for a group, equalling the industry's largest ever advance for a group, which EMI, then the UK's most powerful major label — had recently put up to sign The Yardbirds in a hotly-contested bidding war. It is safe to assume that the EMI advance for The Yardbirds did not arrive in a brown paper bag.

Soon after Immediate landed the Small Faces Jimmy Page quit the label, having decided to join The Yardbirds. The last straw, he later recounted, was when he tried to get the label to sign a songwriter he was keen on, Cliff Ward[66]. Page said he had gone "rushing in to see Tony Calder", really excited, "but Calder just wasn't interested. Not because he didn't like it but just because he wasn't into signing unknowns."

In industry terms the heavily reported Small Faces deal established Immediate as far more than just a hobby-horse for the Stones manager and all but destroyed Decca (the UK's second biggest label) as a contemporary force.

A *Melody Maker* article headlined "Small Faces in Big Record Tie-Up" talked about a lucrative long-term deal for the group "who will in future produce all their own

---

66. Clifford Thomas Ward (1944–2001) was an English singer-songwriter, best known for 1973 album *Home Thoughts*. He had hit singles with 'Gaye' and 'Scullery' but his reluctance to tour may have affected his chances of more substantial mainstream success.

records". Oldham was keen to stress that he would in no way be involved in the production of the Small Faces' recordings which were "solely the group's responsibility", adding: "The group is embarking on a joint publishing venture with Immediate Music, getting songwriter's contracts." The *NME* called it one of the "most important label changes this year".

Decca released a Small Faces single they had in the can, 'I Can't Make It', but with no backing from the group it peaked at No.26.

Looking back Marriott later claimed: "We wanted to go to Immediate because Oldham offered us every freedom besides being a management company. Their interests were selling records and nothing more than being a record label. They knew that if they let us loose and gave us the reins then we could write better material and last longer. Oldham knew we could and would write stuff that lasted forever which, quite frankly, a lot of it has and still will. They were very shrewd people in that sense. It was a good move. It was such a big family thing up at Immediate, all helping out at each other's recording sessions. There were only about four or five acts on the label, admittedly all charting, but only a handful of people were responsible for it all, so everyone got to know each other very well."

The first result was the Summer '67 single, 'Here Come The Nice', Immediate's 50th single — and the label's best-selling since Chris Farlowe's 'Out Of Time'. Recorded at Olympic Studios, produced and written by Marriott/Lane, it spent ten weeks in the Top 40, peaking at No.12. This overt tribute to a well turned-out drug dealer had escaped BBC censure and represented a fantastic return to form for both the Small Faces and Immediate.

Decca attempted to cash in by releasing a collection of early Small Faces' material on the LP *From The Beginning — The Small Faces At Their Best Yet!* Immediate sought an injunction and then hurriedly completed basic recordings of fourteen new Marriott/Lane tracks, and, within a week, rush-released their own Small Faces' album, *Small Faces*, an understandably patchy affair that nonetheless showed great potential.

Immediate also splashed out on an advertising campaign for the album to eclipse that of Decca's, announcing: "Whichever way you look at it, there are only four Small Faces. But there is just one Small Faces LP. It's on Immediate."

Innovative promotional copies of the album, featuring hook exerts from the songs and DJ John Peel spieling hype about the band, were sent to DJs, journalists and record shops, and *Small Faces* became Immediate's best-selling album to date, cruising into the Top 10 and easily outselling the rival Decca effort.

Immediate spared the Small Faces from their usual gruelling live schedule that had seen them play every toilet up and down the country under Arden, and encouraged them just to live, create and be who they wanted to be. As much as Immediate promoted itself as a young, maverick company, this was almost a brave new adult world. It was unheard of at the time for a record company to give an act a block of hash and allow them "to go off for six weeks and come back with the masterpiece they had in them" with the only proviso being "have fun getting it done". The Small Faces had previously been in a world where three days was the norm to create an album.

Marriott spread more joy: producing one of his new songs '(Tell Me) Have You Ever Seen Me' with a new band, The Apostolic Intervention, for Immediate. The band's 14-year-old drummer Jerry Shirley[67] had caught Marriott's eye and a couple of years later would be the drummer in his

67. Jerry Shirley (1952-) is also known for his work with Fastway, Alexis Korner, Billy Nicholls and Syd Barrett, appearing on Barrett's debut LP *The Madcap Laughs (1970)* with David Gilmour and Roger Waters.

post Small Faces band, Humble Pie.

Jerry Shirley: "I was playing in a band with my brother on guitar called The Little People. Steve had sung our praises to Andrew who was interested but didn't like our name. Steve suggested The Nice. He was always saying 'nice', which usually meant nice gear [marijuana], you know. Anyway, we all thought what a great name but Andrew had other ideas. He announced in mock dramatic voice, 'I think you should be The Apostolic Intervention'. We thought, 'Uuugghh, what's that?' but reluctantly we said, 'Okay', and then five minutes later, he decided to call PP Arnold's backing band, The Nice.

"Oldham brought us into his office, sat us down, gave us a huge stack of black [US] records and said, 'Here, snag some of this and come back when you've learnt it'. I was only 14 years old; mouth open, going 'Wow!' On a daily basis I sat in the Immediate office watching all these astonishing people coming and going; Andrew, Mick, Brian... it was nothing short of remarkable. There was a stack of Brian Jones' guitars in the music room at Immediate, Gibson Firebirds, all rusted with blood all over them.

"I was down at Olympic Studios, doing some things with Steve as part of a possible Andrew Loog Oldham Orchestra thing, I look up and there's Jimi Hendrix staring at me. Steve was like showing me off, 'Here you are, check this guy out'. Hendrix said Steve's guitar solo on 'Whatcha Gonna Do About It' was one of his favourites."

With the Small Faces on board, and once their initial two-year distribution deal with Philips had expired, Oldham and Calder took the opportunity to sign a more lucrative distribution deal with EMI who paid a £50,000 advance for a three-year tie-up. Philips would soon be taken over by Dutch company PolyGram and the German light bulb firm Siemens, with a new UK record label, Polydor, created to 'compete with' — but ultimately supersede — the old Philips imprint.

It was hoped that the deal with EMI would allow Immediate to capitalise on its UK success across Europe, something the label had been unable to do with any consistency via Philips. Immediate were "going international" and "getting our own logo throughout Europe" as Calder put it.

Oldham said: "Frankly Philips were very good to us. They gave us our break and without [Philips' MD] Leslie Gould's help we would never have got started. If they had not given us the break that got us off the ground we would never have got the deal we have today with EMI."

Before a record had even been released Oldham set the tone: going loco at an EMI sales convention, he may have put sleeping pills in the canteen soup tureen and got so out of it he ended up chasing an EMI executive down the stairs with a gun and a wooden plank with nails in it.

Tony Calder remembers: "We opened up our first sales conference with a slide of the EMI building with a lump of shit against it. We said, 'We're not a company that throws shit against the wall'. We did all that… but what did you expect us to do? Ken East was the Managing Director of EMI UK and Oldham had a good relationship with him."

It was chiefly due to EMI's new Managing Director that the relationship stayed largely on course for the next two years.

Ken East: "Immediate were the first major independent, they had huge success. The company had an aura about it. Immediate was the independent company of the day and they wanted to do funny things, which of course they did. The dog shit thing? Oldham was ahead of his time in that sense wasn't he? Shock marketing, this was 1967. Things were a lot straighter up and down than they are today. Oldham was certainly different, some people loved him, and some people thought he was a nutcase but Immediate made good records and we were in the record business. EMI were competing for Immediate. They were new, very new, they were at Philips but we were able to persuade them they could do better with EMI.

"At EMI, Immediate had their own stock risk out of necessity because they created the record. They should know better than anybody how many they needed to press and how many were going to be sold. If they said press 5,000 of this, they were responsible for the manufacturing costs and they were kept in our warehouse. When they were sold, we shipped them and we would collect payment from the retailer: if we collected £1 from the dealer, we kept 20 per cent for ourselves and gave the rest to Immediate. If the record didn't sell, they were still Immediate's records, they took the stock risk. You got crazy things from Oldham and Calder; one big spender was bad enough but the two of them together was just dynamite."

To celebrate the EMI deal there was a new Immediate slogan unveiled: "Happy to be a Part of the Industry of Human Happiness". This was printed prominently on single sleeves and has become synonymous with the label.

Immediate PR Andy Wickham went to work for Lou Adler in LA so a new Immediate head of promotions, Ken Mewis, Oldham's hairdresser, was appointed. Mewis reported monthly to EMI's Manchester Square offices, presenting new product to the EMI sales reps gathered from across the UK. The staff list at Immediate was growing fast; another publicist, Ray Tolliday, and a new receptionist, Mick Jagger's recent ex-girlfriend Chrissie Shrimpton. Meanwhile Cynthia had left, pregnant, but there was a new staff lawyer and Company Secretary, Timothy Hardacre, to keep things tight. Hardacre parodied his pinstriped profession to perfection and the press photo of him, Oldham (still disguised in exquisite Irving Thalberg-style *Last Tycoon* attire) and Calder, to announce Hardacre's appointment made for a great image.

Timothy Hardacre: "I first met Tony Calder in 1963 when he had TR Ltd — a PR company doing press for

The Mojos, Swinging Blue Jeans, Searchers and The Undertakers. He had one room in the top of a building in Poland Street. Two guys ran it, one was Tony, who was also DJing at the Lyceum and other Mecca ballrooms. Tony introduced me to Oldham in '67. He was highly unstable: he had just fallen out with David Jacobs, the most famous show business lawyer in London, so I guess I was the replacement.

"Immediate had a very simple contract with EMI, two pages; I went up to the boardroom to meet with the chairman, before Ken East. His first words were, 'How much money do you want?' I asked for £30,000, he said, 'Right' and wrote the cheque.

"Oldham thought he was immortal. They all did. I once went to serve a writ on Don Arden for Immediate. He said, 'Writs! This is what they mean to me!' and he threw them in a cabinet on top of a great pile of other writs. He said, 'Now I'm gonna throw you out of the window'. Then he said, 'Sit down and have a drink'."

Getting High

Immediate had made "enormous strides" in its second year according to a *Record Mirror* recap. "Despite the mushrooming of dozens of new independent labels, Immediate still ranks as the pace-setting independent which other breakaway operators envy and try to emulate."

Oldham and Calder were interviewed at length for the *Record Mirror* feature, the pair revelling in innovations: a new Immediate film lauded to be premièred at the EMI's autumn sales conference.

The "creative, impulsive" Oldham and the "quieter, calculated" Calder said they were undaunted by the loss of the recently outlawed pirate radio stations Caroline and London that had played such a huge role in breaking many Immediate hits. "We rely just as much on the BBC," said Calder, "and we feel that good product will get away even without the pirates."

"Personally I think the whole recording field is wide open in Britain right now," added a newly-bearded Oldham. "We give our acts total freedom because this is the only environment in which people can create properly," added Calder, "Steve Marriott of the Faces likes our set-up so much he says it's like being back at school again. It really took us 18 months to find out exactly what we wanted to do and where we were going wrong. We are dealing with artists and writers not just records and we feel that this is the only way to operate — trying to encourage people to use their own ideas."

Oldham reflected: "I suppose our biggest failure was in not consolidating Chris Farlowe's success after his No. 1 hit with 'Out Of Time' but we still don't feel we've lost him. He can get into the charts with the right material at any time." Neither of the "two latter day tycoons" would admit to having made massive money out of Immediate and its associated publishing, production and management companies. "We had ploughed a great deal back into the company to build it up," insisted Calder. The coming months — Oldham and Calder told *Record Mirror* — would see Immediate focus more on albums and the two were "very pleased" with a new policy of packaging LPs in sealed polythene which they were convinced would "give the consumer greater faith in purchase".

They also planned to continue their innovation of sending out "sampler LPs" to main dealers — as first witnessed with the Small Faces' debut album on the label — and explained how, ten days before any of their artists appeared in a town, they would be sending publicity material for displays in dance halls and record shops.

The pair also revealed they were lining up a major European tour for Immediate artists to "consolidate the label on the continent". They also launched a new book business, with titles set to include *The Immediate Success Story*.

Peter Whitehead, who had shot *The Little Bastard Immediate* promo film, was partner in Immediate Publishing. He was working on the Immediate/EMI promo film too. "For *The Little Bastard Immediate*, I remember Oldham asked, 'How much?' I said, '£2,000' and Cynthia wrote a cheque out there and then. For the next one it was just Andrew saying, 'Hey listen Peter, we're having these sales conferences, I want you to string a load of film together, bung all the various groups together'. Immediate was: now, addiction, the present. It was actually a deliberate attempt to snub the institutions, even though Andrew very surreptitiously used the big companies to make all his money, he still didn't really tow the line.

"We called the film, *Here Come The Nice*. Oldham said, 'Listen, the guys wanna film in Camber Sands, we're all

leaving on Friday at five in the morning; Small Faces, PP
Arnold, Twice As Much'. We set off; I was sitting in the
back of Andrew's Rolls Royce with him and Tony, by the
time we got to Camber Sands we were stoned. I was so
stoned I couldn't see through the fucking camera. I think
the idea was to film the new Small Faces' single 'Itchycoo
Park' as dawn was breaking. There was no time at seven in
the morning to get the instruments together, so we just stuck
them all in the sand and started filming. The whole thing,
as far as I was concerned, was a total catastrophe. I didn't
think I had shot a single foot of film that was usable. By the
time I got back and stuck it all together none of us thought
it was terribly good, it was never properly finished. A rough
cut was shown to all the salesmen.

"My publishing company, Lorimer Publications, did
screenplays. We bought a load of rights off various film
directors, and did something on Che Guevara, made *Benefit
Of The Doubt* with the Royal Shakespeare Company about
Vietnam. Andrew manufactured and distributed them; he
put up the money. For a year and a half they financed it all
and it became Immediate Publishing. We even published
some books together, all based on cinema. Then I took
it back because somebody came along and offered me a
better deal. I went back to Andrew and Tony and said,
'Listen guys I think I've got a good deal with Andrew
Sinclair, I want to go off and do it as Lorimer again'. They
said, 'Okay, whatever'.

"I found both Andrew and Tony extremely easy to deal
with; we never had a single piece of paper between us. We
just understood each other and got on very well. He and
Tony were the odd couple, like Laurel and Hardy; they
complemented each other very well. I don't think you could
have got two madder people than Andrew or Tony at the
time. The offices were near to where I lived in Soho and I
think Andrew saw himself as an Arab prince surrounded by
a harem or something."

The Immediate European package tour lasted 20 days and whistled through Germany, France, Holland, Belgium, Luxembourg, Sweden, Austria, Switzerland and Italy. EMI had offices in each territory and Immediate worked diligently to bring them all on board, knowing their support would determine whether future Immediate releases in each country would get a proper servicing. They also made their own links with television, radio and press in each territory, with Europe's top pop television show, Germany's *The Beat Club*, coming out in total support. The show featured at least one Immediate artist on a weekly basis. Further support came from Emperor Rosko's Radio Luxembourg show, recorded in Paris and broadcast across Europe.

Tony Calder: "We would do these junkets of Immediate acts around Europe and as we were coming into land, Oldham would stand up and say, 'We're in Italy, the only words you need to know are Fuck off in Italian'. We would come off the plane everywhere, any country, shouting, 'Fuck off'. Seriously, we made EMI's whole European operation come alive. It made EMI, who had all these companies in every territory acting independently, suddenly start to operate as a unit. EMI knew what we had done, they did appreciate it and they let us get on with it. They never said, 'You've gone too far'.

"There was a guy in Germany at EMI, English guy, Ian Groves. Oldham comes up and says, 'Hey nice to meet you', and starts taking a piss against the fucking guy's limousine. The name of the game was if you don't promote nothing happens. We promoted. We taught everyone how to promote artists, not just the records but also the artists. Even then we were making television promo films, short videos of artists miming to songs. We took new acts like The Nice and started breaking them around Europe, for us it was the natural thing to do but nobody else thought so."

Ken East: "It's true. When I first came into the overseas division, they wouldn't even talk to each other. The people in Belgium wouldn't talk to the French and the Germans wouldn't talk to the Dutch and it was part of my job to make them do so. I used to have to almost bash their heads together. When we got Immediate for Europe, it became a huge success and success binds people together and Immediate definitely contributed to the unity of EMI's European music companies."

Mike Leckenbush, producer and director of Germany's *The Beat Club*, was reputedly introduced to illegal substances by Immediate and, subsequently, wanted a monthly delivery. Then David Skinner, of Twice as Much, began a liaison with Leckenbush's personal assistant, so Twice As Much appeared on *The Beat Club* more than any other Immediate act — if there was no single they would do an album track. As a result their new single 'True Story' was a Top 10 hit in Germany (and Holland and Switzerland).

David Skinner of Twice As Much told me: "I remember with Plonk [Ronnie Lane] of the Small Faces on the tour we went through a craze of painting our boots with eyes and cottages with smoke going up our ankles. It was just one big binge, just this sort of drug and alcohol ridden haze of music and great times. You used to do a lot of miming; you basically mimed to your single or your hit. That was it; you were on for about three minutes. So people tended to be very out of it on those occasions, you didn't have to sing or do anything, just sort of look alright. As long as you could un-stick your mouth it was all right. We did take a lot of medication. There were very powerful forces at work in terms of creativity. The drugs helped.

"Oldham was like a walking clinic and the acts on Immediate obviously dug him a lot. I remember having some really good times in the studio with Steve Marriott and Ronnie Lane, coming in and doing backing vocals and everybody really grooving and having a great time together, there was a lot of laughter. Tony was more like the guy in the tie, with the button-down shirt and the haircut, and he seemed to be more New York, whereas Andrew was more LA. I think a lot people found Andrew very encouraging, he was very supportive of his acts. Chris Farlowe used to have this irritating habit of ad-libbing between just about every line, 'Yeah baby', and shit like that, we used to laugh about that. Andrew had a knack of having Chris laugh at it too, it was very funny."

In Milan, Oldham was fed up with answering questions from reporters so chauffeur Eddie and Ken Mewis took turns at playing Oldham while he slept. According to a source it was always risky taking Chris Farlowe to Germany for television, radio and press, as you would turn your back and he was off to buy Nazi memorabilia (Farlowe's collection of wartime mementoes would grow over the years and he would end up opening a shop in Islington called Out Of Time to sell it).

Steve Marriott was inevitably thrust into the limelight as Immediate's new great white hope, especially now Jimmy Page had gone. He was 20, dating PP Arnold and Chrissie Shrimpton. Impudent and irresistible: with Jagger and Richards facing a high-profile trial on drugs charges, Marriott delivered a new single, 'Itchycoo Park', which in his own words had a "Walt Disney-sound" and a none too subtle pro acid/marijuana lyric.

Marriott made hay at Olympic Studios, in the leafy London outskirts of Barnes. Olympic had begun life behind Selfridges on Oxford Street in a disused synagogue, and was now considered the premier independent facility in the country, housing two recording studios, One and Two. Oldham had booked both around the clock, at £25 an hour, and made the rooms available to any of the Immediate acts while also encouraging the beginnings of a new Stones album here too.

George Chiantz, engineer at Olympic studios: "There was great excitement when the Stones showed up at the studios. The Small Faces were in at the same time, I think Bill sang on one of their tracks or they sang on some of the Rolling Stones stuff. Steve said Keith wanted him to replace Brian Jones in the band. Andrew was in and out of Olympic all the time, with the Small Faces and PP Arnold, doing demos for a panoply of Immediate artists.

"The one thing I will say is, and it was characteristic of him, Steve Marriott would always push you those 20 minutes beyond which you could not go. So you wound up hating him. You just couldn't stay awake any longer and he would say just do a backing vocal or another mix. If you had an all night session with Marriott you were not going to get out until they had already set up the studio for the next batch of musicians. You could not get him out of the studio, he just loved it in there."

Tony Calder: "I got a phone call from Stevie one night from Olympic, two in the morning, he says, 'You've got to hear this, it's a smash. Where's Andy?' Steve always called him Andy. Steve said, 'Do yourself a favour, get hold of him, this track's got phasing on it'. I said, 'What the fuck's that?'"

'Itchycoo Park' — utilising the new studio technique of 'phasing' and written and produced by Marriott/ Lane — met with initial resistance from the BBC, who considered banning the record because of it's "I got high" lyric. Immediate issued an official statement: 'Itchycoo Park' is a story about a park in the east end of London. It's a slum area similar to the slums of Brooklyn. There isn't any green grass in this park. It's just a strip of wasteland with swings, a sand pit and a hill (the band got high on the swings as kids Calder explained to me). At the bottom of the hill there are loads of stinging nettles (thorns). Kids used to ride their soapboxes off the hills into the stinging nettles and get all itchy. Hence the name Itchycoo Park. There is also a little pond where the ducks land, where the kids feed the ducks."

The BBC quickly backed down and adverts for the single featured on the *NME* front page depicting four small children, one of whom was Eddie Piller[68], in overgrown parkland scrub holding an upside down Itchycoo Park street sign: the only clue to the record being advertised as Immediate entered a new graphic era.

Ronnie Lane would later explain his thinking behind the track: "Andrew had a lot of influence over us because we were very impressionable and he was very moody. He would swan around in his shades and his limousine and he was quite amusing really. He had this camp humour and that's when we started to do these little cameos like 'Itchycoo Park'. Had Andrew known it at the time, of course, he would have probably have demanded a royalty payment."

The single turned in phenomenal figures: 250,000 in the UK; the Small Faces' biggest UK hit for a year, peaking at No.3. It went on to surpass all previous chart achievements for the group, the same amount again, across Europe, top five in Holland and Belgium. It was also No. 1 in Australia and in America a breakthrough for the group, No.16, selling more than 350,000 in the US.

In interviews to promote the hit, Marriott said the Small Faces were planning to tour the US. "We've got a new label in the States, CBS," he raved. "That's a good label to be on out there and we're very hopeful. That's where Andrew comes in again. You know what happened to us previously in the States? They released 'All Or Nothing', 'Sha La La La Lee' and 'WhatchaGonna Do About It' and decided we

---

68. Born in 1962 in Essex, Piller's father ran a firm of bookmakers and his mother ran the Small Faces' fan club during their early years. By the 70s Piller became interested in the punk scene, and was a fan of Buzzcocks before following the Mod-revival of the late '70s. During the early '80s, Piller began DJing at Mod club nights with great success and set up his first record label aged just 21 and later founded the Acid Jazz label that sparked a whole new scene.

were an R&B group, so we got restricted airplay. I mean R&B? We're more a Walt Disney sound."

The CBS deal came as a result of Oldham helping out pals Lou Adler and Mamas & the Papas star, John Phillips, with the organisation of the Summer of Love 1967 Monterey Festival. He was introduced to CBS President Clive Davis at the festival and quickly inked a deal to distribute Immediate in the US for an advance of $100,000. Oldham signed on the line in New York, at the CBS head office on 77th Street, allowing CBS exclusive US rights on Immediate product for two years with a third-year option.

It was a massive advance, one that more reflected Oldham's status with the Stones, than the real worth of Immediate. Trade magazine *Cashbox* called Oldham "a musical giant", and for *Billboard* he was one of the top five record producers in the world. Lou Adler also made a deal with CBS for his new label, Ode, and it was he who had introduced Davis to Oldham.

At Monterey Oldham had suggested booking The Who and Jimi Hendrix for the three-day festival, which attracted 100,000 people to the small coastal town between San Francisco and LA to, the blurb ran, celebrate "music, love and flowers". Flowers were the symbol of the festival, 100,000 orchids were distributed among to the crowd, and a poem called *Flowers* written by Oldham featured in the festival programme.

Brian Jones was the only Rolling Stone to attend, accompanied by Nico, and the two stayed with Oldham and his wife Sheila, at a rented house nearby. Jones was supposed to introduce a few acts alongside MC Mickey Dolenz of The Monkees who was dressed as a Native American for the occasion. Mamas & The Papas, The Animals (whose singer Eric Burdon had relocated to San Francisco), and Simon & Garfunkel were the major draws to the festival, with support from unsigned San Francisco band the Big Brother Holding Company, featuring Janis

Joplin, plus The Byrds, Jefferson Airplane, Otis Redding, Ravi Shankar, The Grateful Dead, Hendrix and The Who (whose awesome auto-destruction antics launched them in the US: four months later they scored their first US hit 'I Can See For Miles').

CBS Records President Clive Davis said he had "an awakening at Monterey"[69]. As well as signing Adler and Oldham, he paid an astounding $250,000 for Janis Joplin and the Big Brother Holding Company in a deal brokered by Dylan manager Albert Grossman. CBS was the Tiffany/ Rolls Royce record label in the States. Davis was already sitting on Dylan, Simon and Garfunkel, The Byrds and Barbra Streisand. Now he was intent on turning the label into a rock powerhouse and, alongside Joplin, he signed up Blood Sweat And Tears, Santana, and Chicago.

Oldham stayed on in LA after the festival to work on a 'Summer of Love' offering from the Stones for the US market, *Flowers*, their ninth US album, cobbling together a compendium of mostly previously unavailable (in the US) Stones' material and a few hit singles. Oldham used the LA graphics team, Tom Wilkes and Guy Webster (who had been responsible for the Monterey Pop Festival packaging), for the cover art. The album peaked at No.2, staying on the charts for an incredible 35 weeks.

Immediate staff recall Oldham flying back from Monterey in a kaftan and a cowboy hat stuffed with flowers and scattering petals all around. He put out an *NME* advert to promote Scott McKenzie's 'San Francisco (Be Sure To Wear Flowers In Your Hair)' on Adler's Ode Records, which became the talk of the trade and Immediate staff plugged and promoted the McKenzie record faster and

---

69. Brooklyn born Clive Jay Davis (1932-) had enjoyed a meteoric rise through CBS from junior legal counsel to President of CBS records within seven years. In the wake of Monterey it wasn't only Davis who enjoyed "an awakening' as, following the signing of all this talent, CBS doubled its market share over the next three years.

better than EMI (who distributed the record in the UK).

Davis flew Immediate's entire creative team to New York to meet with CBS department representatives. He told *Billboard* he wanted to "further Oldham's career as a record entrepreneur", guaranteeing "CBS could sell more albums than any other company in the US for Immediate".

'Itchycoo Park' was swiftly followed by the American release of a Small Faces' album, *There Are But Four Small Faces*. Bruce Hinton, the newly appointed manager of sales and promotion at CBS who now handled both Immediate and Adler's Ode records, was keen to for the band to visit.

But there was a hitch. For some reason the Small Faces were denied entry into America. As an apology, Immediate provided CBS with a film of the band, shot in Chiswick Park, miming to 'Itchycoo Park'.

It's All Over Now

Tony Calder: "The Rolling Stones got resentful of Monterey. Andrew was in a world of his own. He was happy; he was working, doing the press calls with Lou. He was out of his box but for the first time away from the fucking pressure of the UK police, not knowing where to sleep at night. He was like the person I first met."

There had been discontent brewing between Oldham and the Stones since the end of 1966 when the single 'Have You Seen Your Mother Baby, Standing In The Shadow' performed disappointingly in the US, spending only four weeks in the charts and peaking at No.9. Keith Richards broke ranks first to insist that the wrong mix of it had been released. "The original track was fat and fantastic," he told the *New York Times*. In the UK, following seven consecutive No. 1s, the single peaked at No. 3.

Oldham failed to cap the matter, telling the press, 'Have You Seen Your Mother Baby, Standing In The Shadow' was "about the attitude that exists between parents and their children. The shadow is the uncertainty of the future. The uncertainty is whether we slide into a vast depression or universal war."

Later, in an interview with music monthly *Rolling Stone*, Jagger stated: "The single, 'Have You Seen Your Mother?' was like the ultimate freak-out. We came to a full stop after that. I just couldn't make it with that anymore; what more could we possible say? We couldn't possibly have kept it up like that. You just drain out totally. It was the end of a certain period and we had to stop. We had done it; there was nothing more we could do. We just had to wait until we had organised ourselves, and you know, things had changed."

Looking back Richards said: "Suddenly in late 1966 we were so exhausted that we couldn't go on the road. We were wiped. It was a pressure cooker."

With the unwieldy title, feedback-drenched backing and impenetrable lyrics, 'Have You Seen Your Mother Baby, Standing In The Shadow' heralded headlines in the UK such as "Have The Stones Gone Too Far?" and "Stones: What Went Wrong?"

Allen Klein predicted in the press the group would gross an astonishing $20 million in 1967 but between follow-up single, 'Let's Spend The Night Together' and album *Between The Buttons* there was a six-month silence from the Stones with no gigs or releases.

'Let's Spend The Night Together' was a major triumph for Oldham. The basis of the track had been recorded at RCA studios in Hollywood before further work in London, at Pye and Olympic studios. Oldham had overseen a beautifully blended, perfectly balanced mix of piano and guitar, with Charlie's drums leading the charge and was justifiably proud at having successfully steered the Stones toward a fuller, smoother, more mature sound, after the over-the-edge assault of 'Mother'. "Even the backing harmonies were smooth," Oldham joked.

However, promoting the single during a star turn on *Sunday Night At The London Palladium* — ITV's premier family entertainment show — the Stones had done the unthinkable, refusing to wave goodbye with the rest of the show's cast at the end of the programme on a revolving stage. The stage wave was a long-standing tradition of the show. Having been out-voted when he told the band the programme was too establishment for them, he thought, at least, he had communicated to the group that if they were going to appear, they may as well go all the way. There was a very public, violent, stand-up row between Jagger and Oldham on stage at the Palladium over the issue. Comedians Dudley

Moore and Peter Cook, held up a Gerard Scarfe[70] painted impression of the group for the spinning finale but by then Oldham, close to tears, had turned his back and walked.

'Let's Spend The Night Together' peaked at No.3 in the UK and the Stones flew to New York to promote it on *The Ed Sullivan Show*[71], another massive Sunday evening television event. Here the sexual demands laid down in the lyric caused the show's producers to insist that the chorus line of the single be altered. Years later Jagger would claim he did not comply and mumbled his way through the line rather than sing altered lyrics (but it's clear he sung the alterations, rolling his eyes and singing "Let's spend *some time* together").

There was also a danger — Klein told Oldham — that the single would be banned by radio stations in the US over the lyric. Loathe to let go of the controversy and fantastic feel of 'Let's Spend The Night Together', Oldham allowed himself to be persuaded by Klein that the single's flip side, 'Ruby Tuesday', was the best song for US radio. Klein was proved right when 'Ruby' went to No. 1 in the US.

The album *Between The Buttons* went to No.2 in both the US and UK in its first week, kept off both top spots by the latest pop craze, The Monkees. A result of cumulative recording in Hollywood, Pye and Olympic Studios, the *NME* review praised Oldham, who had produced for the Stones "an album richer than ever before in terms of

---

70. Gerald Anthony Scarfe CBE (1936-) is an English cartoonist and illustrator. He has worked as editorial cartoonist for *The Sunday Times* and illustrator for *The New Yorker*. His other work includes graphics for rock group Pink Floyd, particularly on their 1979 album *The Wall* as well as the opening titles of *Yes Minister.*
71. *The Ed Sullivan Show* ran on CBS from June 20, 1948, to March 28, 1971, and was hosted by New York entertainment columnist Ed Sullivan. The Stones performed on the show six times: 25th October 1964, 2nd May 1965, 13th February 1966, 11th September 1966, 15th January 1967 and 23rd November 1969.

variation of pace, sound and excitement".

It seemed as if the Stones, with a new sound and a policy of saying no to all interviews via a newly appointed PR, Les Perrin[72] (an old-school charmer who had looked after Count Basie, Duke Ellington and Frank Sinatra), had ridden out the first hints of a backlash in the UK.

Then the *News of the World* printed a sensational pop star drug *exposé* claiming Mick Jagger had admitted to taking LSD, Benzedrine and marijuana in a story written by Mike Gabbert who had broken a football betting scandal in 1962 that would see several First Division players banned for life[73] and would go on in the 1990s to edit *The Sunday Sport*.

---

72. Born in Manchester, Perrin had a peripatetic career before he ended up in Tin Pan Alley, "in a small office Billy Cotton managed to acquire for me." From then Les managed publicity for the likes of Tony Blackburn, Lulu, Herman's Hermits and Jimmy Young. He handled Nat King Cole, Louis Armstrong, John Barry and when American super stars like Sinatra and Dylan came to the UK, Perrin would inevitably be there to assist. Of the Stones Perrin commented, "They are natural story-breakers. Sometimes for better, sometimes for worse."

73. The British football betting scandal of 1964 saw ten professional players convicted. A Scottish lower league player, Jimmy Gauld, was the ringleader - in late 1962 he approached Sheffield Wednesday player David Layne, a former team mate at Swindon, to identify a target game and he suggested that Wednesday were likely to lose their match on 1 December 1962 against Ipswich Town and suggested to team-mates Peter Swan and Tony Kay that they ensure the outcome. The three all bet against their own side in the match, which Ipswich won 2–0. Kay had the highest profile of those convicted. He was transferred to Everton a few weeks after the game in question and helped them win the league that season. He was also an England international and expected to be in Alf Ramsey's 1966 World Cup squad. Although his life ban was lifted in September 1973, Kay never returned to professional football and later spent twelve years on the run in Spain for selling a counterfeit diamond. Ironically, Kay had been named man of the match in the game that the *Sunday People* newspaper accused him of having "thrown".

Gabbert was hell-bent on exposing the Stones but, in his haste to do so, had in fact cornered the fast-disintegrating Brian Jones in a nightclub, and it was he who had openly confessed to taking the drugs cocktail. Jagger made matters worse by announcing on *The Eamonn Andrews Show: Live From London*, that he intended to sue the *News of the World*. In time-honoured gutter press tradition, reporters from the paper vowed to hound him and the Stones until they had further sordid revelations that would kill off the libel action. The paper had the advantage of working in conjunction with the police who were forming new drug squads to crack down on high profile figures in the pop music scene and despite The Beatles singing the praises of LSD on their single 'Strawberry Fields', the police had marked the Stones down as top of the hit list.

Oldham had warned Jagger, Richards and Jones that strutting about in outlandish "druggy" clothes from the newly flowering King's Road boutiques and flaunting their wealthy, degenerate lifestyle, sent out the wrong message. He knew a drug conviction would mean the withdrawal of visas to the US.

In early February 1967, tipped off[74] by *News of the World*, the Sussex police swooped on a party at Richards' Redlands country retreat in West Wittering. A quantity of heroin, amphetamine and marijuana was found and Jagger and Richards were arrested and charged for possession. "Drug Squad Raids Pop Stars' Party," claimed the *News of the World* spread merrily.

On one level their arrest befitted the image Oldham had so assiduously created for the Stones and maybe he should have been delighted: he wasn't. Whispers started coming back from friendly policemen, via Les Perrin, warning Oldham to watch out, because the police were

---

74. Who in turn were alleged to have been tipped off by Keith Richards' chauffeur.

after him too[75].

In his stead Allen Klein took centre stage in the Jagger/
Richards court case, making a big splash by flying into
London and telling *The Daily Mirror,* "Their problems are
mine. I'm working my ass off to get them the best lawyers
and will be in the front row of the trial every day". Klein
privately advised Oldham that, should Jagger or Richards
get jail time, there needed to be enough Stones' product
to tide them over, or at least a single to ride on the back of
public sympathy should that happen.

Oldham had been having terrible problems getting all
five Stones to show at Olympic studios to record. When
they had, the sessions had produced nothing of worth, and
at times it seemed as if they were playing deliberately badly
to wind him up. Oldham persevered, managing to finally
get the basics of a new single, 'We Love You', together.

Tony Calder recounts: "I remember the Stones came
in to Olympic one night when they were out on bail and
they were doing 'We Love You' and it was a dog. [John]
Lennon came in and said, 'Set the mic up' and he goes in
and puts the falsetto voice on. I had tears in my eyes; it was
magic. That made the record. It was phenomenal."

Oldham added prison doors clanking shut to tag onto
the end of the single if the two Stones were convicted and
organised a short promo film to be ready for *Top of the
Pops*. Directed by Peter Whitehead, it was shot in a church
in Essex and featured Marianne Faithfull, Richards, Jones
and Jagger acting out the trial of Oscar Wilde.

When the sensational news came that the verdict on
Jagger and Richards were not guilty, everyone presumed
'We Love You' was a guaranteed No. 1 but the BBC

---

75. It is claimed that, fearing arrest, Oldham disappeared to the
US for three months. Tony Calder later commented, "I never saw
a man pack his bags so quickly. He was terrified." Oldham's alleged
'desertion' has been touted as the reason behind his Stones sacking.

banned Whitehead's film and the Stones were unprepared for television or concerts. The single peaked at a disappointing No.8 and the album sessions at Olympic were still going nowhere.

The situation at Immediate exacerbated the discontent brewing between Oldham and Jagger/Richards. Calder told me that having been refused part ownership of the label, Jagger was reluctant to produce or promote Immediate in any way.

Oldham was still just 23 when it was announced he and the Stones were going their separate ways. They'd shared the most incredible four years any of them would ever have, that any group would ever have. Les Perrin delivered the official statement: "The Rolling Stones have parted from their recording manager because the band have taken over more and more of the production of their own music. Andrew Oldham no longer has any connection whatsoever with the Rolling Stones."

Mick Jagger added in *NME*: "I felt we were doing practically everything ourselves anyway. And we just didn't think along the same lines. But I don't want to have a go at Andrew. Allen Klein is just a financial scene. We'll really be managing ourselves. We'll be producing our own records too. I shan't continue to produce for Immediate; it was all so draggy. The biggest disappointment is not doing Pat Arnold's records." More recently Jagger has said: "The reason Andrew left was because he thought we weren't concentrating and that we were being childish".

Oldham told *NME*: "Everything the Stones have done has been natural. They were not puppets; they were people. Whatever else is said about them they were as close to professional as any five artists can get. We split because we had no need of each other anymore. As people we went in different directions. There was no definite decision. It was just over. We just weren't on the same wavelength anymore. We had gone as far as we could together. It was time to move on."

The divorce was made messy when Oldham's original co-manager in the group; the greying, old-school showbiz agent, Eric Easton[76], sued for half the Stones' income to date in a £1 million High Court litigation. Oldham had hooked up with him 1963, when he was 19 and needed office space and someone with an agent's permit to book the Stones' gigs (arcane laws meant you needed to be over 21 to apply for this permit). Easton was dropped by Oldham after just a few months and had done nothing of note for the group, especially over the past couple of years. Nonetheless he pursued a prison committal order against Oldham "for failing to comply with an undertaking to produce a list of documents or to pay into an account money he received in respect of their three years of joint management of the Stones".

Whenever Easton's lawyers came knocking at Immediate, Oldham would nip out onto the second-

---

76 Eric Easton (1927-95) was born in Rishton, Lancs and started out as an organist in venues such as local cinemas and with his own ensemble, Eric Easton and his Organites. He later described his business partner Oldham as having "something of the Hayley Mills" about him. Easton was in charge of bookings in the early Stones career and his close relationship with Dick Rowe was key to the band signing to Decca. Easton wanted to model the group on Beatles lines and organised the band's chaotic first US tour before ALO finally ousted him in 1965.

In October 1971, he launched a series of lawsuits for breach of contract against the band, Oldham, Decca, London Records, Allen Klein and Nanker Phelge. As a result, the High Court froze a million pounds-worth of the Stones' UK assets until the case was concluded. Decca was also instructed to suspend all royalty payments to the group. Easton eventually settled for $200,000.

Bill Wyman later said of him: "It's easy twenty-five years later to put a guy like Eric down as a boring old-time agent who didn't understand what young tigers like the Stones were driving at, but he worked hard and well for us."

floor roof and dive next door through Dick James' office window, and a stooge would happily accept the paperwork. The dispute over the three-year Oldham/Easton co-management agreement on the Rolling Stones — signed when Oldham was just 19 and Easton was in his 40s — was settled when Allen Klein took control of everything, paying Oldham and Easton both an estimated £700,000.

Would You Believe (I Loved You Yesterday)

In the aftermath of the split with the Stones, Oldham displayed increasingly violent mood swings; sackings at Immediate often involving a quick upturning of the desk. He was in the New Oxford Street office most days; casting a half-opened eye over administration with Calder and waiting until the normal stream of talent trooped in before lunch and camped there for the rest of the day as lunch turned into tea.

There were wild nights out with theatre designer Sean Kenny who, with his down-to-earth Irish wit, entertained and educated, leading Oldham to see the possibility of new worlds and adventures. The pair often drank together at Fulham Road's Trencherman and together they came up with a plan for Kenny to design the stage for a 'Love-In', the UK's answer to Monterey, featuring PP Arnold, new Immediate group, The Nice, Donovan and Pink Floyd.

Privately Oldham was struggling. £700,000 was a handsome pay-off, and he still held a sizeable interest in the publishing on Jagger/Richards songs but there had been something else between him and the Stones, particularly Jagger and Richards, some alchemy which had produced a monumental body of work. He confessed to Kenny he often felt suicidal and had been suffering from recurring bouts of depression. A similarly "redundant to requirements" Brian Epstein had recently committed suicide, at the age of 32, from an overdose of barbiturates (leaving The Beatles managerless until Allen Klein stepped in).

Kenny recommended his psychiatrist Dr Mac (Doctor

Luke McLoughlin) who also treated Tony Hancock[77], Hank Marvin and Jet Harris from The Shadows. Dr Mac diagnosed Oldham as suffering from manic depression and put him through a treatment of electric convulsive therapy, with electrodes attached to his temples and a device placed in his mouth so that he could not shatter his teeth or bite off his own tongue when 180 to 460 volts of electricity would be sent through his brain, often rendering him unconscious. Oldham also spent weekends at Hampstead's Bethanie Nursing Home, where Dr Mac would administer a Deep Sleep Treatment, putting him into a sort of coma for days, held down with a combination of barbiturates, sedatives and the latest psychotropic drugs on the market.

If Dr Mac hadn't knocked Oldham out and there was nothing on television, chauffeur Eddie would take him to cabaret clubs in the Phantom 5 to see acts such as Bob Monkhouse, Frankie Howerd and Shirley Bassey. Sometimes Oldham would fall asleep before he got there and later ask Eddie if he'd had a good time. Eddie would reply, "Yes it was okay" or "You were totally out of order".

The show went on at Immediate and acts that got to see Oldham always left happily stoned on whatever was the flavour of the day, usually having forgotten the reason for their visit; artistic discussions, money or just to chat. There were more new staff at New Oxford Street now; Steve the messenger, a cockney likely lad, would run errands and deliveries on his moped. Jim Watson was recruited from EMI and promptly had his desk upturned by Oldham for looking like a dummy from a Burton's window. Keith Lewis was recruited from EMI for a marketing position but was

---

77. Anthony John Hancock (1924–1968) was an English comedian and actor. Hancock killed himself by an overdose, in Sydney, on 25 June 1968, he was found dead in his Bellevue Hill flat with an empty vodka bottle and a scattering of amylo-barbitone tablets.

far too straight to cope with Immediate for longer than a couple of months and joined A&M Records as General Manager. There were other diversions: one afternoon three new E-Type Jaguars pulled up outside the Immediate offices and Oldham leant out of a window to pick a colour.

Eventually he got back to work in the studio, excited about producing a new Immediate signing, Del Shannon, whose early 1960s rock 'n' roll chain of hits — 'Runaway', 'Hats Off To Larry', 'Little Town Flirt', 'I Go To Pieces' — had been favourites of Calder and Oldham. Oldham had met Shannon, who was recording for Liberty Records in the US (but going nowhere with current producer, Tommy 'Snuff' Garrett) in London at a BBC show.

Del Shannon: "Al Bennett was the president of Liberty. I called him and said, 'Andrew Loog Oldham wants to produce me, he's expensive, he goes into the studio with top cats'. We had 25, 30 musicians. So for three or four weeks I had the time of my life with Andrew. He let us use his Rolls. I liked him because he was very adventurous. He wasn't in a good place in those days, 'cause of the break-up with the Stones, but I liked him and I liked working with him musically. He did it all. I just said 'take over', and that's a dangerous thing for an artist to do, unless the guy really knows what you're doing and knows your style."

Oldham recorded Shannon at Olympic Studios utilising the talents of John Paul Jones, Nicky Hopkins, PP Arnold and many more Immediate regulars on songs he had selected from the growing Immediate Music song catalogue.

Jeremy Paul, one of Immediate Music's staff songwriters (and a childhood pal of Oldham's): "I wrote a song called 'Mind Over Matter' and played it to Andrew. He said it was 'wicked'. At that second he phoned Del Shannon and played it to him over the phone. Del flipped, he said, 'I'm coming over right away to record it'. They took him to Olympic Studios. I get a call about one in the morning,

'Jeremy it's Andrew, get down to Barnes now, Del can't sing the top note'. They had got Del Shannon high as a kite. I went out on the floor; I write in falsetto, I write for females, this was a girl's song. I screamed at the top of my voice. Del got the note. I think they speeded up the track. I wrote this song 'Would You Believe'. PP Arnold recorded a version that went Top 10 in Italy. I met Andrew in the south of France when he was 16 and I was 15. We used to mess about on this little £10 Woolworth's harmonium at my parent's place down there. I kept it and had used it on some of my demos. When the Small Faces were doing *Ogdens' Nut Gone Flake* they insisted on using this harmonium."

Unfortunately, contractual details prevented Immediate releasing the Shannon material in the UK and in the US Liberty did not consider it in keeping with Shannon's image and shelved it. The tracks were re-appraised, to great acclaim, 20 years later when the album was issued on CD.

In these chaotic, drug-fuelled times, also recording for Immediate were former Manfred Mann singer Paul Jones, Madeline Bell[78], *Hair* star Linda Kendrick[79], Buffalo Springfield member Neil Young (who was said to have cut a track for the label, produced in London by Oldham/Jack Nitzsche), David Bowie, Jethro Tull and the Chris Brough managed Ayshea[80], but none released any official product on the label.

The Small Faces kept themselves busy, in the studio

---

78. Madeline Bell (1942-) is an American soul singer who rose to prominence in the UK with pop group Blue Mink and contributed backing vocals on the Stones' 'You Can't Always Get What You Want'.
79. Linda Kendrick (1951-2010) was known for appearances in *Z Cars* (1962), *Mike and Bernie's Scene* (1970) and *4-3-2-1 Hot and Sweet* (1966).
80. Ayshea Hague, (1948-) was a regular on TV in the 60s, she made appearances on *Thank Your Lucky Stars* and *Discotheque* as well as *Jason King* and *UFO*. Granada TV hired her to host her own pop show, *Lift Off with Ayshea* in 1969, the same year she married her manager.

working with Billy Nicholls[81], a new good-looking teenage signing to Immediate. He recorded Jeremy Paul's 'Would You Believe' as a single (produced by Marriott and Lane) and used the same name as a title for his debut album. Nicholls was friends with Cat Stevens, having worked alongside him and Elton John[82] at Dick James' office.

At Immediate Nicholls, like all the acts, was put on a weekly wage, £20 a week, with he said his "own room full of Revoxes, Mellotrons and the Stones' guitars". The *Would You Believe* album featured heavy involvement from Marriott on guitar and vocals, Cat Stevens on piano with Jerry Shirley from Apostolic Intervention on drums, and all the regular Immediate session crew: Nicky Hopkins, John Paul Jones and Art Greenslade. Despite a great advertising campaign and an astonishing sound, there was little demand for the album and a follow-up single, the Nicholls penned 'It Brings Me Down', with a video shot in Piccadilly Square, stiffed. However *Would You Believe?* is now one of the most sought-after albums on Immediate, an original vinyl pressing of the album reportedly worth £1,600[83] [2015 figure].

---

81. William Morris Nicholls Jr (1949-) is an English singer, songwriter, composer, record producer, and musical director, his father Billy Nicholls (Sr.) being a double bassist and big band singer. His compositions have been covered by many artists, notably Leo Sayer's version of 'I Can't Stop Loving You (Though I Try)' which reached No. 7 in the UK Singles Chart. Nicholls wrote several of the tracks for the film *McVicar)* including 'Without Your Love', which was a success in the United States.

82. In 1967, Elton [then Reginald Kenneth Dwight (1947-)] answered an advertisement in the *NME*, placed by Ray Williams, then A&R for Liberty Records. At their first meeting Williams handed John an unopened envelope of lyrics written by Bernie Taupin (1950-) who had answered the same ad. John wrote music for the lyrics and then sent it to Taupin, beginning a partnership that still continues.

83. According to www.discogs.com the record could be worth as much as £8,000 (2023).

Mike d'Abo[84] was another young songwriter freshly signed to Immediate Music. Having replaced Paul Jones[85] as lead singer, following a run of eight Top 10 hits such as 'Do Wah Diddy Diddy' and '5-4-3-2-1', d'Abo had lead the Manfred's into a more adventurous with material such as 'Semi-Detached Suburban Mr James' and 'Pretty Flamingo' and he'd just scored a No. 1 smash in the UK with 'The Mighty Quinn'.

Despite the group being signed to Fontana, there was nothing to stop d'Abo from writing his own songs for Immediate Music. Soon after signing, he wrote 'Build Me Up Buttercup' for The Foundations, which sold in excess of three million copies worldwide. Oldham and Calder were happily convinced that in d'Abo they had their very own Jimmy Webb, the new hot writer in the US who had scored with 'Go Where You Wanna Go' and 'Up, Up and Away'.

"They gave me the names of two singers they wanted me to work with," remembered d'Abo. "Rod Stewart and Chris Farlowe. I had never actually heard of Rod Stewart[86] until they mentioned him to me." Stewart had been signed up to Immediate since early 1967 and, like PP Arnold before him, had been waiting for the right song to record. He had already cut a single for Decca, 'Good Morning Little Schoolgirl', and recorded a version of Sam Cooke's

---

84. Michael David d'Abo's (1944-) career following the Manfred's break up in 1969 saw him play Herod on the original recording of *Jesus Christ Superstar* and a short role on the original recording of *Evita*.
85. Paul Jones, born Paul Pond, (1942-) began his career as a blues singer with various bands before being asked by Keith Richards and Brian Jones to be the lead singer of a group they were forming - he turned them down. Following success with the Manfreds, Jones enjoyed a long TV and radio career as a presenter and acting roles in shows as diverse as *The Sweeeney*, *Space: 1999* and *Evita*.
86. By 1967 Stewart was not a complete unknown. In '65 he had toured with the Stones and The Walker Brothers with blues outfit Steampacket and in '66 joined Peter Green and Mick Fleetwood in Shotgun Express.

'Shake' for EMI. Now, after a brief stint with Long John
Baldry's Steampacket, he was occasionally singing with
London blues outfit Shotgun Express.

   Tony Calder: "I remember Rod first coming into my
office and feeling: 'This guy's got it!' I actually saw a star
in front of me. Andrew and I loved him. But at the time
Mick [Jagger] was jealous. Rod was pretty and younger.
Jagger said, 'You like him don't you?' Andrew and I replied,
'Of course we do. He's going to be a superstar'. Before
Oldham broke up with the Stones, we talked Mick round
and persuaded him to produce Rod's debut single for
Immediate but, as the time neared, he pulled out. There
were also plans to have PP Arnold and Rod record an
album with Jagger producing but they were scotched when
Mick threw a tantrum and said he was not going into the
studio."

   Calder forgot that Jagger had, in fact, made it to the
studio for a session with Rod early in 1967, with Keith
Richards, Nicky Hopkins and PP Arnold also present.
They cut a cover of 'Working In A Coalmine'. Stewart's
early manager, Geoff Wright, recalled a row in the studio,
"with Mick saying Rod could not hit the high notes, and
that his voice wasn't right for the song". In the end d'Abo
wrote and produced Stewart's sumptuous piano-driven
Immediate debut, 'Little Miss Understood', with the Small
Faces helping out in the studio. The resulting single had a
colour sleeve, portraying Stewart himself in a moody pose
and his name emblazoned across the top; but sales-wise it
was not a success, only selling 263 copies in the UK.

   Rod next recorded a duet with PP Arnold on the Barry
Mann/Cynthia Weil song 'Come Home Baby'. His former
long-time girlfriend, Jenny Rylands, was marrying Steve
Marriott and she urged her fiancé to write a hit for her
former beau. "Marriott wrote some incredibly commercial
things for me to record," Rod said later.

   Immediate tried to convince their US distributor, CBS,

of Stewart's potential but 'Little Miss Understood' was never released in the US. Six months later, Stewart joined The Jeff Beck Group as did Immediate session man Nicky Hopkins. They both enjoyed considerable success in the US with the Jeff Beck album, *Truth* — released on the CBS-owned Epic label, selling approximately 160,000 copies.

The prolific d'Abo also provided the song for Chris Farlowe's next single, the plaintive 'Handbags and Gladrags', which put the singer back in the charts, peaking at No.23 and, after 'Out Of Time', would become his most celebrated Immediate outing. 'Handbags and Gladrags' would be later resurrected by the band Stereophonics and used as the theme tune to BBC television comedy *The Office*.

PP Arnold's former backing band, The Nice, released their debut Immediate single, 'The Thoughts of Emerlist Davjack', written and produced by 'Emerlist Davjack'; a name conjured from segments of the four band members' surnames. Compared with what was to come from The Nice, the single was fairly straight psychedelic pop. The group debuted live in front of a 60,000 strong crowd at The National Jazz and Blues Festival in Windsor Great Park and followed that with a residency at the Marquee Club, a series of gigs so successful the band wrestled house records from such luminaries as The Jimi Hendrix Experience, The Who and Stones. The group became renowned for their great live shows, with extended organ led outbreaks of freeform madness. *Melody Maker* hailed them as successors to Eric Clapton's Cream: "Their music is wholly unlike any being played by another modern pop group — in Britain or America," the paper swooned. "It is violent, often neurotic, yet rich in chords, harmonies and melodies. They improvise as spontaneously as a jazz group, they are as free as a psychedelic group, but with vastly superior instrumental ability."

The Nice starred on a UK package tour alongside Jimi Hendrix, Pink Floyd, Amen Corner and The Move, and the group's organist, Keith Emerson[87], was on his way to becoming an unlikely star. In America, critics were also full of acclaim for the group following showcase gigs at the Scene in New York, Whiskey A-Go-Go in LA and the Fillmore West in San Francisco.

---

87. Keith Noel Emerson (1944–2016) was a classically-trained pianist who became fascinated by jazz in his teenage years and went on to transform the role of the keyboard in rock music. After adopting the Moog synthesiser he formed Emerson, Lake & Palmer in 1970 with bassist Greg Lake from King Crimson and drummer Carl Palmer from Atomic Rooster. Renowned for overblown adaptations of classical symphonies, Emerson became synonymous with the prog sound which dominated 'serious' music in the early 1970s.

When Emerson moved to Santa Monica, California in the mid-90s, John Lydon, who had openly and harshly criticised ELP during the 70s, was Emerson's neighbour. The two became friends, with Lydon saying in a 2007 interview, "He's a great bloke".

Ogdens' Nut Gone Flake

Oldham's love for the unstoppable enthusiasm of Steve Marriott flickered back to life. He described the Small Faces frontman as "the best of Mick and Keith in one vibrant soul". Marriott delighted in leading Oldham to enjoy a different rhythm of life. He jokingly called Phil Spector 'white faggot music' and forced American soul and Stax onto the play list in the Immediate offices, a selection of Bobby Bland, Rufus Thomas, Larry Williams, James Brown and Solomon Burke.

Having lost interest in the Top 10 in the fug of the Stones' ending, Oldham was pleasantly surprised to find that the UK had never had it so good: with songs such as 'Heard It Through Grapevine', 'Your Precious Love', 'You Make Me Feel Like A Natural Woman', 'Higher and Higher', 'Never My Love' by The Association and 'The Letter' by The Box Tops (led by 16-year-old Alex Chilton[88]), all riding high.

Inspired, Oldham, who had purposely kept a low public profile since the Stones split (not wanting to be pointed out as "the ex-Rolling Stones manager") decided he'd had enough of playing Howard Hughes, got his hair styled into a Carmen-rollered Afro, matching the perm with a beard, Braggi Bronzer make-up (supplied by Bloomingdales in New York), eyeliner and shades. His wealth was apparent in the handmade suits, glittering rings, cuff links, bracelets

---

88. William Alexander Chilton (1950–2010) was best known as the lead singer of the 60s pop act the Box Tops and later Big Star (1971-74) a band that foreshadowed the style of alternative rock of later decades and is frequently cited as a seminal influence by influential rock artists and bands.

and watches he flaunted.

Oldham would spend 45 minutes on his new hairstyle each morning, while Eddie rolled the first joint of the day. Oldham would then look out of the window, select a car from his fleet, and be in town at Immediate's office by ten, once more happy to be a part of the industry of human happiness.

NME feature writer Keith Altham, who had handled so many Stones' features in the past, was an early invite to the Immediate offices to listen to Oldham's new groove, an advance hearing of the Small Faces' new single, 'Tin Soldier'. Written and produced by Marriott/Lane, the song had originally been intended for PP Arnold but she had been so blown away by it the Small Faces had second thoughts and kept it for themselves. Arnold sang backing vocals on the track and did the same on the many television appearances undertaken by the group to promote it. "'Tin Soldier' is the real us," Marriott told Altham, adding that 'Itchycoo Park' was really just "a nice kind of send-up." Marriott also talked of a UK tour in the spring and spoke of his continued desire to go to the US if 'Tin Soldier' followed 'Itchycoo Park' into the charts.

The Small Faces had disappointed by being unable to promote themselves in person in the US on the back of the huge success of 'Itchycoo Park'. Calder bluffed it was due to "unbelievable demand in Europe" but it was rumoured the band were having trouble getting working visas for the US as keyboardist Ian McLagan had been busted for possession of dope. McLagan remembered the situation differently in his memoirs: "We should have gone over to the US when 'Itchycoo Park' was in the charts. The problem was we weren't tight on stage. Once we had the freedom in the studio, we just cut out most of our live playing."

In an early 1968 edition of *NME* Keith Altham (who would go on to be the Stones' PR in the 1970s) wrote of his visit to Immediate: "Once more unto Andrew Oldham's inner sanctum off Oxford Street to interview his group Small Faces and discuss the fate of 'Tin Soldier' with songsmiths Steve Marriott and Ronnie Lane. It was just like old times when music, laughter and sarcasm were the hallmark of many a colourful interview with another known group that Andrew managed. When I made my entrance (one cannot simply enter Andrew's office as you walk through and onto a raised balcony) I was not totally prepared for the *Alice In Wonderland* tea party scene that unfolded before me. Gambolling about the office were two lanky Afghan hounds and a black and white collie of doubtful pedigree. While seated around the table were Steve, Ronnie, Andrew and a journalist left from a previous interview. He [the journalist] was apparently asleep and remained affixed to his chair throughout the interview. In beautiful green tumblers on the table was Black Russian, a delightful drink."

Altham: "Immediate was intuitively very clever. Andrew had enormous flair and he knew talent when he heard it. He knew a face when he saw one. David Bowie was doing stuff for Immediate around that time. Oldham was terrible, he was rude, obnoxious, bad-tempered, he humiliated people, and he was dreadful. Andrew and Tony used to sit in this white office behind this double desk painted white with all these white phones. The two would whisper into each other's ears. It was rather disconcerting to say the least; you would wonder what the hell they were talking about. You would ask a question and they would start mumbling to each other. I asked Tony about this, years later, and he said it wasn't about anything at all; they used to do it deliberately just to put people off."

The hard, heartfelt 'Tin Soldier' hit the Top 10 in the UK and blazed up the charts around Europe and the world. In Australia, where 'Itchycoo Park' had been a No. 1, the single raced in to the Top 10. Oldham, Calder, the Small Faces and co-headliners, The Who, jetted out to Australia for a two-week, 20-date tour in January 1968 arranged by Harry Miller, The Stones' Australian promoter. The Who had just released their *Sell Out* album and Pete Townshend had begun work on an ambitious rock opera but the Small Faces were the bigger pull and closed the shows.

The group were, however, badly under-rehearsed, a sub-plot of the visit was to tighten them up for live UK dates. At Sydney Stadium Marriott walked off stage in a strop, kicking off about the low-quality gear the band were playing with and was disconcerted when the venue's famous revolving stage got stuck mid-way through the group's set. The Who, who had been touring since their triumph at Monterey, were a much tighter unit on stage, if just as volatile, and it was soon agreed that they would close the shows.

The Aussie media hated The Who and the Small Faces, with particular offence taken at the "screaming of obscene four-letter words on stage". Townshend had to be held back from punching one reporter who dubbed the tour, nominally called *The Big Show*, 'The Pig Show'. One daily newspaper urged fans to boycott concerts describing the Small Faces as "weedy, bumptious, arrogant, sulking, sneering ambassadors for Britain", accusing them of inciting riots, adding "the 8,000 fans who had bought tickets at $3.60 (AUS) a head" were being ripped off by the "scruffiest bunch of Poms[89] that ever milked money from this country's kids".

The newspaper attacks, reminiscent of the Stones' first visit there, amused Oldham, as he recovered in a

---

89. The most common explanation for the Australian insult 'Pom' in reference to anyone English, is that it's a reference to Australia's past as a convict colony. "Pom" is supposedly a bastardised acronym, meaning "prisoner of Mother England" or "prisoner of Her Majesty", another is that is a shortened version of pomegranate whose ruddy complexion is similar to immigrant Brits.

Melbourne hospital following an altercation with a security guard at a gig in the city. Prevented from going backstage, tempers frayed, with Oldham insisting he was about to show the crowd the "greatest lighting show Melbourne had ever seen" before being sparked out.

Landing in Sydney, before transferring to a connecting flight to New Zealand, the entire touring entourage were greeted on the runway by armed police. The captain of the plane had radioed ahead complaining of "beer swilling" and abuse. Although the air stewardess who had made these complaints later admitted to exaggerating her story (and was sacked) the incident set a precedent for a week of madness in New Zealand, made infamous by the party organised by Harry Miller and EMI (who distributed Immediate down under) for Steve Marriott's twenty-first birthday in Wellington.

Presented with a portable record player and a stack of records, Marriott (stoned and drunk) threw another of his tantrums. He later recalled: "I still remember the track, 'Baby Don't Do It', a Marvin Gaye track that Stevie Wonder did a great version of. Then the record player started to feedback on itself. So I bunged it out of the window and off the balcony, it was a mad moment. It was the highest building in Wellington, one of the high-rise hotels. So Wiggy (a roadie for the The Who), ran down, brought it back up, all in bits and throws it off again. Well, it was the wrong thing to do in front of Keith Moon, because the next thing that went out was the telly, armchairs, the whole lot went out of the window, the whole room. It was dumb because the groups didn't do that then. I don't think anyone had done it. There was an audience watching us down below, so we thought, 'What can we do?' So I said, 'I know, let's ring up and say someone's got in our room and destroyed it, say they've nicked a couple of guitars to give the story a bit of credibility' because we thought, 'Fucking hell, we can't own up to this'. So we rang down and the police and management came up and, incredibly, we got away with it. Then EMI presented me with a proper stereo and the hotel spent all day putting new French windows and doors on this suite and new furniture gets put in.

"Come the evening Keith came up again and he said, 'They've done a good job haven't they?' Then bosh! He's done it again, put another chair through the French window, he's going, 'Yes yes yes', bunging things out and smashing things. The whole room was fucking wrecked again. Now we can't get away with it and it also makes us look like right liars from the time before. The hotel manager is banging the door. Keith looked at him and said, 'I fucking did it!' They brought in the police but we got them pissed. Instead of doing their job and keeping us under control they ended up going mad, drinking all the brandy. We were all wearing their big white helmets, dancing about. Well, they brought in the army after that. They had these geezers outside each one of our doors in short trousers with bolt loaders like fucking big Lee Enfield muskets. You would open the door and they would go, 'Get back in there' at gunpoint and that's a fact. So New Zealand was glad to see the back of us as well."

It cost Immediate a small fortune not only to compensate for hotel damages but also to stop any further action being taken by New Zealand authorities (Oldham ended up losing around £10,000 on the tour) but nothing could be done to stop Marriott's increasingly temperamental behaviour. He walked off stage again in Auckland, screaming "this fucking piano's out of tune". He was also hostile toward the rest of the group, particularly his songwriting partner Ronnie Lane. At the time, Lane was said to be on Marriott's back over his predilection for handing out their songs to other Immediate artists when he felt they could be better used by the band.

Tony Calder: "Steve says to me, 'I'm not going on with that arsehole [Ronnie Lane] again. I'm not having that cunt nick my money anymore. He's never written a fucking song, he treats me like a piece of shit, and I'm not finishing this fucking tour.'"

The Small Faces flew back to London with Australian newspapers bidding them good riddance: "Both bands are unwashed, foul-smelling, booze-swilling no-hopers and we don't want them back again!" Pete Townshend made a pledge never to return down under and — despite massive financial incentives over the years — has kept his word.

Oldham turned 24 in Australia. Despite the hospital visit he'd enjoyed the sunshine break, topping up his tan and organising water-skiing classes at every opportunity (Keith Moon's idea of a joke had been to cut the rope as soon as the boat skipper announced there may be crocodiles in the area).

The bills on the Small Faces' eagerly anticipated new album had been allowed to pile up and it was long overdue. After almost six months of on and off recording at Olympic studios, Immediate urged them to complete and hired two barges to ferry the group and their partners up and down the Thames for lyric writing sessions.

Of the material Oldham had heard, he particularly rated a track the band were not considering including on the album, with Marriott branding it just 'a joke'. Oldham urged Marriott to reconsider, reminding him of how many No. 1 records had been thought of as a joke by their composers. "Blatant commercialism often scares the act," he told me, saying how the Stones had initially regarded 'Satisfaction' as a "bit of a gimmick".

The Small Faces, like the Stones, decided to listen to their manager, worked a little more on finishing the track and adding toward the finish — as a tribute to Oldham's belief that the song was a national anthem — a take off of the 'Satisfaction' riff. Acetates were sent out to radio DJs to gauge response. It was suggested that the track was missing something. Oldham added bells from the square in Barnes, where Marriott lived, and other atmospherics.

Four weeks later 'Lazy Sunday' was at No.2 in the charts. Steve Marriott's yell of "Fuck the neighbours" managing to sneak by radio censors. 'Lazy Sunday' is a near perfect marriage of hallucinogenics and the musical vaudevillian roots of working-class England, simply one of the greatest rock tracks ever recorded in the 1960s.

Immediate adverts for the single, placed prominently on the front page of *NME*, featured an image of the violent confrontations between students and police at the recent Left Bank Riots in Paris, when 10,000 students took the streets to march against university conditions in an explosion of grenades, street-fires, tear gas guns, water cannons, paving stones and firecrackers.

NME writer Keith Altham was up at Immediate again for a Small Faces interview to promote 'Lazy Sunday' and to hear an exclusive preview of the Small Faces album. He noted Oldham lounging on a black leather sofa looking "like some eastern potentate, in a black and gold embroidered silk robe" and then "beautiful blue crystal goblets were produced and filled with sparkling liquid".

Altham added: "For half an hour they bombarded my senses with sounds from the completed side of the next Small Faces album — and what an album it is. I am sworn to secrecy about the format but can tell you that they have come up with a fantastic narrator to link the tracks and every track I heard was brimful of good fun, excitement and happy music."

The band's keyboard player, Ian McLagan, told Altham 'Lazy Sunday' was "really quite a straight song to begin with until Steve began chucking in 'Rinky Dinky Doos' for a giggle. When we finished it we all thought it was very funny but had no intention of releasing it. We felt 'Tin Soldier' was much more the kind of thing we wanted to do. It was really the enthusiasm of people like Andrew and Michael d'Abo which won us round and we began to think, well maybe everyone else will see it as a giggle too."

'Lazy Sunday' was a huge hit across Europe: No. 1 in Holland, Singapore, New Zealand and Switzerland (where 'Tin Soldier' was also at No.9). It was No. 2 in Germany and breaking in Italy, where the band played their first live dates since Australia. It was part of a hugely successful European tour (also taking in Scandinavia and Germany) where a series of concerts broke all previously established attendance records for venues.

In the UK, praise for the single came from every quarter. *Daily Express* said, "I don't think Immediate has released a bad disc" and *Daily Mail* reckoned, "Small Faces, once the rowdiest beat group, have matured since their association with Immediate into one of the most creative groups in Britain today".

Immediate's Head of Promotions and General Manager, Ken Mewis, was handed the job of delivering 'Lazy Sunday' to the US. He reported back that CBS were not convinced of its potential [previous single 'Tin Soldier' had 'only' sold 35,000 copies in America] and they were unsure when or if they would release it, pointing out the group were still prevaricating over touring (or even just visiting) the country.

Oldham and Calder could no longer hide their dissatisfaction with CBS. In exclusive material from a late 1969 affidavit, recorded when Immediate sued CBS for $7 million in lost earnings, Oldham testified: "After the first six months of our relationship with CBS, not only were Tony Calder, myself and our then general manager Ken Mewis having problems keeping CBS to their promises regarding advertising, promotion, time-buys etc. We were becoming increasingly suspect of their word and version of exactly what was happening to our product in the US.

"As there was no way of checking their reports of activity efforts, response to product via reviews and radio stations, we only had their word to go on. Unfortunately, it had been impossible to maintain the outside promotion men we had hired independently to promote 'Itchycoo Park' by the Small Faces [at a cost of £5,000]. It was a matter of sheer economics, the cost of maintaining these people (who CBS thought unnecessary and would not consider making any contributions to their fees). In fact CBS considered the hiring of them as an insult to their company. Thus, after 'Itchycoo Park' we had only the word of CBS's personnel handling Immediate regarding activity."

Reviewing *Ogdens' Nut Gone Flake* in the *NME*, Keith Altham said that apart from being encased in the first circular sleeve he had ever seen, the new Small Faces album was a landmark for the group, "almost certain to put the group in the same smash album selling bracket as Beach Boys, Rolling Stones and Jimi Hendrix".

The conceptual album fused the Small Faces at their most organic and playful. 'Lazy Sunday' sat alongside bruisers such as 'Afterglow (Of Your Love)', 'Song Of A Baker', and 'Rollin' Over'.

Actor Stanley Unwin[90] supplied narrated links between tracks — the story of a fictional character, 'Happiness Stan' searching for the other half of the moon. One side of the album was to be listened to as a single piece; mixing instrumentals with nursery rhyme and lighter touches ('Happy Days Toy Town').

The packaging of the album matched the quality of the music: a round, multi-layered sleeve ingeniously unfolding to reveal pictures of king size rolling papers and blurry

---

90. Stanley Unwin (1911– 2002), sometimes billed as Professor Stanley Unwin, was a British comic actor and writer who invented his own comic language, "Unwinese", which was referred to in the film *Carry On Regardless* (1961) as "gobbledygook". Unwinese was a corrupted form of English in which many of the words were altered in playful and humorous ways. Unwin claimed that the inspiration came from his mother, who once told him that on the way home she had "falolloped over" and "grazed her kneeclabbers"

Mankowitz shots of the group. The album's title and the package were mischievously adapted from a popular brand of rolling tobacco, Ogdens' Nut Brown Flake.

The sleeve idea was concocted by Immediate one night in Bremen, Germany, after the Small Faces had appeared on *The Beat Club*. Gaining authorisation from different tobacco companies had been a task for Immediate but the ingenious packaging really helped sell the album.

Immediate's PR was sharp too, an advert parodying the Lord's Prayer had certain vicars and Members of Parliament up in arms about the Bible being abused for 'pop' promotion.

The label issued a flip statement, defending the ad: "There has been a lot of comment about it. But we didn't write it. We borrowed it from God. We merely changed the words a bit."

"Small Faces

Which were in the studios

Hallowed be thy name

The music come

Thy songs be sung

On this album as they came from your heads

We give you this day our daily bread

Give us thy album in a round cover

As we give thee 37/9d

Lead us into the record stores

And deliver us *Ogdens' Nut Gone Flake*

For nice is the music, the sleeve and the story

For ever and ever"

A more sedate Immediate advert read: "*Ogdens' Nut Gone Flake* manufactured by Small Faces. Cool, clean satisfying. Firmly packed. Luxury strength. In the unique round packet."

On the first day of release in the UK, *Ogdens'* sold 20,000 copies and the LP smashed into the charts at No.9. Seven days later it was at No. 1 and stayed there for six weeks, staying in the Top 10 for 19 weeks in total, going on to break the 100,000 sales mark in the UK to become Immediate's biggest album to date.

And among stiff competition – the Stones' *Beggars Banquet*, The Beatles *White Album* and Jimi Hendrix's *Electric Ladyland* – Altham's prediction was vindicated when *Ogdens'* was voted "the album of the year" by *NME*.

Steve Marriott: "We cleaned up every award in the book for it and Oldham collected them. We caught him on the stairs of Immediate's office, his arms full of bits of plastic — Best Artwork, Best Design, Best Album."

Pete Townshend: *"Ogdens' Nut Gone Flake* was a world-shaking record. When they first played it to me the only material I had heard to which it could be compared to were concept pieces, like *Pet Sounds* or *Sgt. Pepper*. I was jealous of the Small Faces' sound; they were becoming an extraordinary sonic force to be reckoned with."

"It made us laugh," Marriott said in *Melody Maker*. "Anything that made us laugh we liked. God knows how it worked but it did and I'm very proud of it, and the other Small Faces are too. It was worth the year's work. We didn't know a thing about the Lord's Prayer advert until we saw it in the music papers and frankly we got the horrors at first. We realised that it could be taken as a serious knock against religion but on thinking it over, we didn't feel it was particularly good or bad it was just another form of advertising."

Drummer Kenney Jones told *NME*: "Really this album is just the beginning of things. Before we were with

Immediate our albums used to turn out like sausages. They stuck us against the nearest brick wall and took a photo for the cover. We never really could work up much pride into what we were putting in it with that kind of system. We are getting better lyrics together and better ideas. On stage we use six brass players: trumpets, saxophone and trombones. When we go into the studio now we don't have to worry about wasting half an hour and we recorded some of the tracks on *Ogdens'* perhaps ten times."

With *Ogdens'* another huge Euro hit (selling 110,000 in Germany alone), Immediate staff delivered the album to CBS at the US label's annual record convention in Puerto Rico. Immediate were allowed to show a BBC2 documentary about the making of *Ogdens'* and a short promo film of their own, narrated by Radio 1 DJ John Peel, talking up the album, "a success in every major market outside Japan and the US". The film also puffed up Immediate's other acts: The Nice performing new single 'America' live at the Marquee club and a PP Arnold video for 'Angel of the Morning'. There was also an Immediate biography handed out, based on *The Bible* and split into the New and Old Testaments.

The Immediate presentation concluded with the words: "In ending this, our first Epistle to America, Immediate looks forward to CBS Records repeating the success in the States that the Immediate label has scored with every Immediate artist throughout the rest of the world."

Before flying on to the Bahamas and Antigua in a private Lear Jet, Calder and Oldham presented their US sales and marketing manager Bruce Hilton with a gold disc for his phenomenal success with Herman's Hermits. Hilton was retiring. CBS had put Ron Alexenburg in his place as Immediate's new promotion manager. He redesigned the award-winning *Ogdens'* package for America and pulled the song 'Mad John' off the album as a single.

"We agreed to this," said Oldham, "although we felt that were the track strong enough we would have released it as a single in the UK. The result — another flop."

'Mad John' not only failed to get the airplay CBS promised, but it received no advertising of any importance. *Ogdens' Nut Gone Flake*, Europe's biggest selling and most critically-acclaimed album of 1968, suffered the same fate — no advertising, no airplay — and only managed to shift 25,326 copies in the US, plus a further 5,000 on import, with many retailers reporting they found it easier to get hold of the original UK version than the CBS pressing.

The failure to capitalise on the European success of *Ogdens'* in the US market was a financial blow. The album had cost a huge amount to record and package. Even though European sales were strong, Immediate had hoped for significant revenue from the US to counterbalance costs.

Steve Marriott, who saw many of his contemporaries gaining rich reward in the US, hastily delivered a new Small Faces' single, one he felt would be more in tune with the long-haired, folk-tinged, heavy-rock scene beginning to dominate in 1968 America.

It wasn't what was needed: in his garden at home, a mansion set in five acres of leafy Buckinghamshire, he recorded 'The Universal' on a tape cassette. This version of the song, despite several attempts at Olympic, could not be bettered. Only a gentle trombone and clarinet hook were added to Marriott's garden guitar and vocal. It meant the sound of his dogs barking, and his wife Jenny greeting him as she came back from shopping, stayed on the recording. "Recorded in 30 minutes," Marriott boasted.

'The Universal' peaked at a lowly No.16 in the UK charts and, worse, it was never released in the US. "When it wasn't a hit in a big way it was considered a mistake and it killed me," Marriott said. "I didn't write again for a long while. The disenchantment that comes, even from the rest of the guys, when things ain't a hit, is a crippler. I just went apart in the head."

Marriott was unwilling to take *Ogdens' Nut Gone Flake* on the road in Europe, and the few UK live shows the group did to support 'The Universal' were disappointing affairs. Marriott was thinking of breaking up the band, trying something new.

He told the press: "Pop audiences have changed. Once it was screaming all the time when we were on stage. There's nothing we like better than a crowd of kids rioting, punching bouncers, pulling down walls and hitting each other. Kids come now and expect to sit and hear the sounds on our records, and of course we can't do it on stage. We've been doing college gigs in Britain and the audience here are all so way above it. They only like you because you happen to be 'in' at the moment — they don't understand what the hell it's all about. It's sad. Bring Back Violence!"

America (7 Min. 20 Secs.)

After the success of 'First Cut Is The Deepest', which had sold approximately 40,000 in the UK to go Top 20, PP Arnold had been working Europe consistently and her follow-up single 'The Times Has Come', sold a respectable 20,000 on the continent. Now she was breaking out again with a song Marriott and Lane had written and produced, 'If You Think You're Groovy'. The b-side of the single was a track from the Immediate vaults, 'Though It Hurts Me Badly', by PP and produced by Mick Jagger.

With the rollicking 'If You Think You're Groovy' climbing the UK charts, Arnold was eager to promote it, and herself, in the US. CBS said not to bother; they had been unable to rouse any interest in either the single or her debut Immediate album, *The First Lady Of Immediate*, compiled from recordings made in 1967, with Mike Hurst or Mick Jagger producing. Oldham had contributed a more recent production of Spector/Mann/Weil's epic 'Born To Be Together' and promised Arnold he would be taking a more hands-on approach with her career in the future, telling her he was going to make her a cross between Ronnie Spector and Aretha Franklin.

He took her back in the studio to produce a scintillating cut of 'Angel Of The Morning'; the Small Faces solid backing replaced by understated orchestration. The track was arranged by John Paul Jones and written by Chip Taylor, who had also written 'Wild Thing'. It was another hit in the UK, staying on the charts for 11 weeks. The single did get a US release but sold no more than 800 to 1,000 copies and received no promotional push aside from,

Oldham stated in his affidavit, "bulk product adverts".

At Olympic studios Oldham completed the recording of a new PP Arnold album, *Kafunta*. Tracks fell into four linked parts: Kafunta One ('God Only Knows', 'Yesterday', 'Eleanor Rigby' and 'Angel Of The Morning'), Kafunta Two ('As Tears Go By') Kafunta Three ('To Love Somebody') and Kafunta Four ('Welcome Home'). Oldham also re-recorded her on a far superior performance of 'The First Cut Is The Deepest' for a potential second crack at the charts with the song.

"Kafunta is Swahili for soul," Oldham told *NME* as Immediate's packaging of the album came in for special praise. "Worth buying for the cover alone," wrote *NME* of a Gered Mankowitz shot of Arnold with her hair styled to look like a Red Indian headdress. It had been another expensive packaging job yet sales were disappointing. When CBS refused to release *Kafunta* in the US, Immediate bit the bullet and released PP from her contract. She signed to Atlantic Records in America and switched to Polydor in the UK. Her first single in the US on Atlantic was Oldham's version of 'First Cut Is The Deepest', complete with full-page music press adverts. In *Cashbox* magazine, Arnold was named "West Coast Girl of the Week" and Oldham's version of 'First Cut Is The Deepest' was described as "a near classic".

Twice As Much were also released from their Immediate contract after getting the thumbs down from CBS. Their debut single, 'Sittin' on a Fence', had sold 55,000 copies in Europe and 35,000 in the US (via Allen Klein's short-lived deal with MGM). Their three subsequent singles, 'Step Out Of Line', 'True Story' and 'Crystal Ball', had in total sold about 65,000 copies in Europe and the UK, but CBS hadn't considered any "right" for a US release. Twice as Much's final statement, *That's All* (a greatest hits package) which included a version of Mann/Weil's classic 'Coldest Night Of The Year', a

duet with Oldham's early 1965 discovery Vashti — proved
a hit in Europe and sold 10,000 in the UK.

Another Immediate greatest hits album, *The Best Of
Chris Farlowe*, hit the Top 20 in the UK but his new single,
'The Last Goodbye', the title track of a film, written and
produced by Mike d'Abo, failed to capitalise on the success
he'd had with 'Handbags and Gladrags', and Farlowe was
another artist who was stiffing in the US.

CBS had agreed to release Farlowe's version of 'Paint
It Black' as a single, a galloping, violin-drenched Oldham
production, promising full advertising and promotion
(although maybe not; sales were just 1,674). A US album,
Paint It Farlowe sold a total of 1,596 copies.

Farlowe had sold well over half a million singles and
100,000 albums in Europe and, like Arnold, was getting
itchy feet over his failure to make inroads into the US
market. Several of his old UK 'blues' contemporaries, such
as Eric Clapton, were having huge success in the US. "I'm
tired of banging my head against a brick wall," Farlowe told
the press. Immediate released Farlowe from his contract
and, like PP, he signed up to Polydor in the UK and Atlantic
Records in the US.

"We had no alternative but to give Chris Farlowe a
release from his contract worldwide," Oldham stated in his
court affidavit. "CBS's attitude allowed us no way possible to
change Farlowe's label in the US to a company satisfactory
to Farlowe's management/agency and thus allowing us to
retain him through our usual channels outside of the US."

The Nice's debut Immediate LP, *The Thoughts Of
Emerlist Davjack*, featured a great Gered Mankowitz shot
of the group huddled together topless and wrapped in
cellophane. The music deviated wildly from organ-driven
prog-rock to overblown takes on classical (Bach) and jazz
(Dave Brubeck's 'Blue Rhondo A La Turk'). The album
was considered "mind shattering" by *Melody Maker*. The
group were buoyed by many such good reviews. Radio

DJs such as Radio 1's John Peel and a burgeoning underground press were giving them a big push. The group had cemented their underground reputation with a headline grabbing performance at the Festival of Light at Alexandra Palace, an event that also featured The Who and Pink Floyd. Organist Emerson was now making a regular feature of attacking his keyboards with knives.

Oldham took a more hands-on approach with the band: overseeing the recording of a crazed seven-minute instrumental based on 'America', the Bernstein/Sondheim written song from *West Side Story*. Production was credited to the group, as Emerlist Davjack, but Oldham was all over the release. PP Arnold's young daughter delivering the spoken word climax: "America's Government with promise and anticipation is murdered by the hands of the inevitable."

America was rocking from a new assassination in the aftermath of the JFK and Martin Luther King deaths. Presidential favourite Robert Kennedy had been shot dead in June 1968. The Vietnam War was bloodier than ever with Viet Cong suicide squads besieging the US Embassy in Saigon and the US's largest air base in Da Nang and at the Democratic Convention in Chicago police waged violence on war protestors in full view of the nation's news cameras. In the Watts district of LA mass rioting left three dead and 45 injured, evoking memories of the 1965 Watts riots in which 34 lives were lost.

Oldham told the *NME* that "American violence inspired" the new Nice single. "The two sides of America — its violence and its attempt at maintaining calm — are represented on 'America'," was *NME*'s interpretation.

The Immediate advert campaign, shot by Gered Mankowitz, was their most controversial to date: featuring the band and three children wearing masks of JFK, his brother Bobby and MLK. Each small boy sat on a knee of a group member, with a strap-line that read, "It's taken America 475 years to find themselves, and they're still looking. It took The Nice seven minutes 20 seconds".

The advert featured prominently on the *NME* cover, in many national newspapers and in an extensive poster campaign nationwide. It was broadly attacked for being distasteful, but Immediate remained unrepentant via press release: "All forms of communication are an art form and those unable to respect other's expression must condemn themselves. People throughout the world have felt the necessity to express their emotions and thoughts of American tragedies and each person must use the medium of expression that is within his ability. The posters that show everyone the end product of violence will continue to be displayed. The Nice are sincere in their compassion with Americans and will continue to express their emotions through any medium they choose."

'America' was the longest song to make the Top 20 to date, and stayed on the UK charts for 16 weeks, defying all the normal rules of promotion and airplay. But Tony Stratton-Smith[91], The Nice's manager, was not happy. He was demanding "a written undertaking that in future no more of the controversial adverts would be distributed", claiming that the group's bookings and even record sales were suffering as a result.

He told the press: "The Nice feels that if the posters are issued in America, they will do considerable harm. The group has been offered a US college and television tour in September and we have no wish to create ill will from the

---

91. Tony Stratton-Smith (1933–1987) founded the London-based record label Charisma Records in 1969 and later managed Genesis. He started his career as a sports journalist, and while at the *Express* he was assigned to cover the Red Star Belgrade v Manchester United European Cup match in Yugoslavia. However their chief football correspondent Henry Rose pulled rank and decided to go instead. The aircraft bringing back the team, officials and press crashed in what became known as the Munich Air Disaster and Rose was one of the fatalities.

outset."

The controversy surrounding the group grew more inflamed when Oldham persuaded The Nice to burn US army draft cards at a gig at the Marquee club in London and then a large US flag at a charity "Come Back Africa" concert at the Royal Albert Hall in aid of the International Defence and Aid Fund for South Africa, an event part-organised by Sean Kenny.

The US flag burning stunt went through the roof, with coverage across the tabloids. Frank Mundy, manager of the Royal Albert Hall, was reported as saying he had specifically asked The Nice not to include any symbolic burning in their act. Oldham responded in the press by saying: "If Mr Mundy finds that distasteful he should go to the US and Vietnam and see what he thinks of the sickness there."

Keith Emerson said in the papers that he was forced into burning the flag. Stratton-Smith told the press: "The Nice are the last group to need this sort of publicity. The boys don't like it and perhaps Immediate will wake up to the fact that they are something more than a stunt group."

Tony Stratton-Smith later recalled: "Oldham's Immediate was brilliant. They had a marvellous A&R policy. They developed some great artists. But we had the absurd situation where Oldham appointed his personal barber [Ken Mewis] as the general manager of the label. This poor chap was paid to sit there listening to managers' gripes and say he would look into it. I learned a lot of good things creatively from Immediate. With respect to Andrew I don't think he really had any faith in The Nice. I think he totally underestimated what they were about. That's why they brought me in."

Oldham detested Stratton-Smith and soon by extension The Nice. For the cover of *Ars Longa Vita Brevis* (Latin for Art Lives Long and Life is Short), The Nice's second Immediate album, which featured an X-ray of the group with harmless coloured dye in their veins, Oldham joked about replacing the dye with a slow working poison.

Immediate nonetheless worked hard to push The Nice: arranging for a BBC2 documentary to be devoted to the group (the same production team behind the *Ogdens'* doc). *Melody Maker* called *Ars Longa Vita Brevis*: "A major breakthrough in pop group experimentation. The Nice are swathed in great majesty, improvisation and discovery." Elsewhere Keith Emerson was being hailed as the "Jimi Hendrix of the Hammond Organ".

Nik Cohn wrote in *Queen* magazine: "Keith Emerson is the best pop organist in the country, and one of the best in the world." Both *Record Mirror* and *NME* named The Nice as the world's second-best instrumental group of 1968 and Emerson won the Keyboard Player of the Year award from *Beat Instrumental* magazine.

US reviews for the album were even more effusive, calling The Nice the "most significant British group since The Beatles". US shows in San Francisco, LA and New York, further enhanced The Nice's status. At the Scene Club in New York they beat previous attendance records set by The Doors.

Yet when it came to turning that goodwill and grassroots support into record sales in the US, CBS were less responsive than expected. Lee Jackson, the group's bassist and lyricist: "CBS got it into their heads that they would trail release the single, 'America', and they picked of all places Miami, Florida. Now why on earth release a thing like that there in a millionaire's playground, I can't imagine. In fact Andrew was completely amazed, 'What the fuck... Why Miami?' It sold quite well; it did about 25,000 in Miami. I think it just got moved slightly on the underground stations in New York."

A final episode in this seemingly endless struggle with their US distributors finally pushed Oldham over the edge.

Duncan Browne[92] was a 21-year-old singer songwriter newly signed to Immediate. Oldham produced his debut album, *Give Me Take You*. "A very good and poetic LP with a pervading air of melancholy," wrote John Peel in a *Record Mirror* review. Initially the LP seemed to land with CBS who compared Browne to their own acts Bob Dylan, Paul Simon and Leonard Cohen. However a single from the album, *On The Bombsite*, sold just 38 copies in the US; the album not doing much better (selling 985 copies).

---

92. Duncan John Browne (1947– 1993) is best remembered for his moderate hit single 'Journey' which peaked at No. 23 in the UK in 1972, and its corresponding 1973 album *Duncan Browne*, which has since garnered a cult status among fans of 1970s folk rock.

Tony & the Hamburgers

While Oldham licked his wounds, Tony Calder was left to come up with his own solutions on how to run Immediate more economically and productively. He sounded out a deal to license the whole of US label A&M's product for the UK and gave Immediate's European distributor, EMI, six new A&M albums to listen to by artists such as Joni Mitchell, Joe Cocker, Procol Harum and Spooky Tooth, hoping they would put up some of the cash needed to complete the deal but it came to nothing. He also negotiated the UK licensing on 'Bad Moon Rising' by Creedence Clearwater Revival but that too went astray, the hit single ending up on the Fantasy label in the UK. Crosby, Stills and Nash were also interested in being on Immediate for the UK but again this deal failed to materialise. It's safe to assume Calder couldn't get the final okay out of Oldham to make any of these deals a reality.

So Calder took a different approach. A lot of the new UK groups making it big in the US featured guys who had recorded for Immediate in the past, specifically Eric Clapton who had gone massive with Cream and bigger still with his new group Blind Faith. So Immediate re-issued 'I'm Your Witchdoctor', the 1965 John Mayall & The Bluesbreakers single, advertising it as 'featuring Eric Clapton'. Sales were encouraging in the UK and even CBS couldn't deny Clapton had sales potential and released the single in the US to a promising response. Encouraged, Calder cobbled together an album from the Immediate vaults for the US market, *Anthology Of British Blues* which proved to be the label's best-seller in the US for over a year.

"The idea of Mick Jagger and Bill Wyman of the Stones, Jimmy Page of The Yardbirds and Blind Faith guitarist Eric Clapton together on one record may sound somewhat unlikely," ran the press release, "however, on the Immediate album, *An Anthology Of British Blues*, there are several tracks featuring this very line-up. The British blues scene grows stronger every day and for an understanding of the growth and power of the movement this Immediate album is essential. John Mayall's Bluesbreakers have recently scored great successes in the US and have been an institution in Europe for many years. They also contribute several tracks, again featuring the man Clapton who has become a model for guitarists everywhere. The album boasts further tracks by lesser known, but nonetheless vital, Blues groups who contain musicians who have since become deservedly famed throughout Europe. Immediate have earned the public's gratitude with these historic recordings."

In the UK two lavishly packaged compilations appeared, *Blues Anytime Vol. 1* and *Blues Anytime Vol. 2*, released in conjunction with Mike Vernon's Blue Horizon Records (home to Fleetwood Mac and Chicken Shack). The albums featured the early work of the best and biggest names in British blues: Jeff Beck, Cyril Davies, Long John Baldry, Nicky Hopkins, John Mayall & The Bluesbreakers, Jimmy Page, John Paul Jones, Mick Jagger, Bill Wyman and Ian Stewart and Fleetwood Mac's Jeremy Spencer. The stand-out track, 'On Top Of The World' by John Mayall's Bluesbreakers, was again heavily advertised by Calder as featuring Clapton. In fact, Clapton featured heavily on all the recordings, solely credited with tracks such as 'Snake Drive', 'Miles Road', 'West Coast Idea' and 'Tribute To Elmore' and, as co-writer, with Jimmy Page, on 'Freight Loader', 'Choker' and 'Draggin' My Tail'.

How Calder and Immediate came by these Clapton recordings remains contentious. The idea that the songs were secretly recorded on a two-track, reel-to-reel deck hidden behind a sofa at Clapton's house as he jammed with Jimmy Page is part of Led Zeppelin folklore. Whatever the story, these Immediate releases destroyed Page and Clapton's once close relationship. Clapton apparently didn't buy Page's claims that he had to hand over the tapes or he would be sued by Immediate.

Tony Calder remembers: "Jimmy Page would wander in, saying, 'Hey man, I've recorded Eric'. The tape-recorder was never hidden. They used the bathroom to get the echo effect. Jimmy would say, 'Come on Eric we'll go into the bathroom and record these'. I didn't even know what the blues were! I just knew it was something from over there that you put over here and if you put a proper package on it and had these names like Eric Clapton, who were credible, it would sell."

Ken Mewis: "When we needed another name or two to help fill out an album of obscure blues tracks we would call Jimmy Page. He would get an 'out of it' Eric Clapton round to his house and just jam away with a Revox [recorder] running behind the sofa. The next day Jimmy would come into Immediate with the tape and collect £100 cash, saying, 'Call it anything, forget about royalties, just don't let Eric know, if you need a name, use my street address Miles Road'."

Calder began to look at the British Blues series as a classical line, a way of adding depth to Immediate and the albums were hits in the UK, selling in total close to 50,000. In the US, *An Anthology of British Blues Vol. 2* was released, followed by *Blues Anytime Vol. 3* in the UK.

The link up with Blue Horizon records also resulted in Malcolm Forrester becoming the new boss of Immediate Music. Forrester came with vast experience, having worked for Freddie Bienstock's publishing company Carlin and for David Platz at Essex Music. He had now set up his own publishing company, Getaway Music, which held the

Fleetwood Mac publishing rights, hence his involvement with the Blue Horizon label. Forrester pooled his lot with Immediate Music and the Immediate staff went to work on the new Fleetwood Mac single, 'Albatross', helping make it a UK No. 1 hit, even though the group remained on Blue Horizon.

Malcolm Forrester: "Tony Calder phoned and said, 'You've got to run our publishing house, Immediate Music'. I went round there and they had the publishing on so many good things. They had the Beach Boys stuff, Small Faces, all these songs that they owned, all these good writers, stuff by Jagger/Richards, Marriott/Lane, Cat Stevens, Billy Nicholls and Mike d'Abo. They had all the blues stuff, Jimmy Page, Eric Clapton, John Mayall. We decided if we pooled our stuff we would have one of the best publishing houses in the UK.

"I found Tony Calder to be stunningly bright, quite sensational. My office at New Oxford Street was up the far end, right away from Tony and Andrew, it was like my own little department, much more low-key. At the time a play on BBC radio was most probably about three or four pounds on performance income. I remember all the staff in the office being in mohair suits, shirts made to fit; there were no jeans in the Immediate offices.

"It was always a very gentlemanly company, not bloke-ish, none of that, 'Whoa! Check her out'. Everyone worked on the legend of Andrew. When the whole company car thing started in this country, he was waiting on New Oxford Street for a cab to take him somewhere and I came by in my Zephyr Ford with tail fins. I said I would take him. It was on my way home, he's got in and he's gone, quite disgusted, 'It's all plastic inside'. When he got out the car he said, 'Tell Tony he's got to get you a new car'. I was offended. A few weeks later Calder says, 'You've got to go down to Norman's in Mayfair, we just chose a Mercedes for you'. All my young publishing friends in those days were gob-smacked.

"Immediate, as a whole, was stunningly hard working, grafting all the time. It wasn't a lackadaisical place, the reason it was successful was hard work, you could go to the Immediate offices at nine o'clock at night and see the whole office packing records for mail shots. Calder would send out for hamburgers before it was even fashionable. An early night was an eight o'clock finish. Hard work but good fun. I have to say I always thought Chris Farlowe was a lucky bastard, they bought the No. 1 spot with 'Out Of Time', there were loads of better singers around, Georgie Fame, Zoot Money[93], Geno Washington[94].

"One time I was sitting in a booth with Andrew in the Rainbow on Sunset Boulevard. There were two guys with us. When they went I said, 'Who was that?' It was Gerry Goffin[95] and Jimmy Webb — enormous writers at the height of their careers — just sitting there having a beer, chatting."

---

93. George Bruno Money (1942-) is an English vocalist, keyboardist and bandleader best known for his playing of the Hammond organ. Money was associated with The Animals, Peter Green, Steve Marriott, Kevin Coyne, Kevin Ayers, Humble Pie, Alexis Korner, Mick Taylor, and Spencer Davis to name but a few.

94. Geno Washington, born William Francis Washington, (1943-) is an American R&B singer who released five albums with The Ram Jam Band between 1966 and 1969, and eight solo albums beginning in 1976. He was encouraged to make a comeback in 1980 due to the rekindled interest in him resulting from the Dexys Midnight Runners hit single 'Geno' but he declined as he was completing his degree in hypnotism.

95. Gerald Goffin (1939–2014) was an American lyricist. Collaborating initially with his first wife, Carole King, he co-wrote many international pop hits of the early and mid-1960s, including the US No.1 hits 'Will You Love Me Tomorrow', 'Take Good Care of My Baby' and 'The Loco-Motion'. It was later said he had the gift "to find words that expressed what many young people were feeling but were unable to articulate." Goffin and King were inducted into the Rock and Roll Hall of Fame in 1990.

Paul Banes: "When Malcolm joined I went to work for him. On the publishing side we looked after Sea Of Tunes for the Beach Boys, they would have sold over half a million. We looked after Shelby Singleton, a big producer in Nashville. The biggest song I had with Immediate Music was a cover we got with Val Doonican. We sold so many records, 50,000 a day every day before Christmas - 700,000 copies. We had 'Build Me Up Buttercup' written by Mike d'Abo, a huge hit. We had Long John Baldry[96].

"If you were looking at Immediate Music in terms of *Music Week* today, we would have been a top five publishing company at the time. All the songwriters were home-produced more or less. We had 'Albatross' by Fleetwood Mac and the Chicken Shack acts that Malcolm introduced.

"The publishing deals we offered bands and writers were all similar. The publishing with the Small Faces, for instance, we set up a publishing company for them which they called Avakak and it was a 50/50 deal. Mike d'Abo had a company called Michael d'Abo Music.

"The record label was also known for being artist-friendly - new acts came in all the time wanting to sign to Immediate. Status Quo's manager Bob Young came in. They were getting two per cent record royalty with Pye and he wanted to know if we could give them four, five or six per cent, like we were giving our other acts. We were very close with Donovan and he was working with the Small Faces

---

96. John William "Long John" Baldry (1941–2005) was one of the first British vocalists to sing the blues in clubs and shared the stage with many British musicians including the Stones and The Beatles. Before achieving stardom, Rod Stewart and Elton John were members of bands led by Baldry. He enjoyed pop success in 1967 when 'Let the Heartaches Begin' reached No. 1 in the UK. Baldry lived in Canada from the late 1970s until his death. He continued to make records and voice-overs. Two of his best-known voice roles were as Dr. Ivo Robotnik in *Adventures of Sonic the Hedgehog*, and as KOMPLEX in *Bucky O'Hare and the Toad Wars*.

in the studio. All these bands were in the same boat; the majors were still taking liberties.

"The Immediate staff weren't making a fortune. Everybody used to chip in. We would systematically do a mail-out to the fan clubs, Small Faces, whatever, letting them know what was available. Everybody would be there until midnight, sticking bits of paper into envelopes. Tony would nip round the Wimpy bar and buy us all Wimpy and chips."

With Forrester on board, Calder zoned in on Fleetwood Mac. Not content with owning the group's publishing, he wanted to release the follow up to 'Albatross' on Immediate. He moved fast and Peter Green's 'Man Of The World' was quickly in the shops on Immediate. You could say it remains maybe the greatest song Immediate released, certainly the most maudlin.

The advert for it was another Immediate special, taking over the entire *NME* front cover. It depicted a reclining policeman smoking a joint, backed by four golden labradors and an Andy Warhol flower painting. Immediate wanted the 'police officer' to look as stoned as possible, and David Bailey's bill for the photos read: "Fee £500, Props £500 (for authenticity)."

Immediate and Fleetwood Mac seemed a good fit, founder members Peter Green and Mick Fleetwood had played with former Immediate act John Mayall & The Bluesbreakers, and they had a good relationship with Forrester. The group were coming straight from a massive No. 1 single with 'Albatross' and 150,000 sales took 'Man Of The World' straight to No.2 in the UK charts, only unable to top 'Get Back' by The Beatles.

It was announced to the press that Fleetwood Mac planned to record an orchestral-choral album telling the story of Christ for Immediate who began arranging continental gigs for the group. Calder was working on a deal with Immediate's European distributor EMI to bankroll a massive advance for Fleetwood Mac — but somehow things didn't work out as planned.

"I got all the money lined up from EMI," Calder told me. "Quarter of a million quid we lined up, highest UK deal ever done at the time and we're sitting at No.2. Oldham comes out of the treatment centre and has lunch with Fleetwood Mac's manager Clifford Davis. He then calls me and says, 'The deal's off. He cut his roll with the wrong knife. I won't sign the cheque'."

Oldham: "Malcolm Forrester calls and says I've got to meet him at this lawyer's office in Holborn. I alight from the Roller, see Malcolm on the pavement and ask him what's up. He says, 'You remember Fleetwood Mac'. I say, 'Yeah, I met them twice'. He says, 'Well we forgot to sign them'."

Malcolm Forrester: "I had the publishing of Fleetwood Mac and that's how Immediate got them. What went wrong is we had a conflict with Clifford Davis. It's a load of old tosh about forgetting to sign them. Ted Oldman was our lawyer at Immediate and he was Clifford Davis' lawyer. That's a conflict of interest. They were telling us we could not continue with my publishing agreement with the writers of Fleetwood Mac at Immediate Music. Calder was good in these situations; aggressive, sharp and quick. Oldham wouldn't have known what was going on."

Fleetwood Mac's manager Clifford Davis announced the group were leaving Immediate, telling *NME*: "There has been many problems and we have accordingly decided not to sign with Immediate." Davis instead used the success of 'Man Of The World' to negotiate a deal with the US label, Warner Bros Reprise.

A Bomb on the Bus

Clive Davis, President of CBS Records, reputedly worked 18-hour days and knew every detail of his operation, right down to the daily sales figures. A recent CBS album, *The Rock Machine Turns You On*, showcased the impressive roster Davis had accumulated: Bob Dylan, Laura Nyro, Janis Joplin (all three of managed by Albert Grossman), Moby Grape, Blood, Sweat and Tears, The Byrds, Simon and Garfunkel, Taj Mahal, Big Brother and The Holding Company, Leonard Cohen, Johnny Cash, Roy Harper, Tim Rose, The Zombies, Electric Flag, The Peanut Butter Conspiracy, Spirit (produced by Lou Adler), The United States Of America and Grace Slick.

Over the past couple of years, Davis had overseen a doubling of CBS' annual record profits to a figure around the $10 million mark, with his post-Monterey rock signing leading the way. He was a Harvard educated lawyer, a middle-class Brooklyn Jew who, under the old CBS President, Goddard Lieberson, had quickly risen from assistant consul to administrative vice president overseeing A&R. He then became general manager and ultimately the big cheese.

Alongside their new rock roster CBS had deals with leading black labels Philadelphia International and Stax, and Davis was also closing in on the signing of Bruce Springsteen and Billy Joel. He was not a man known to take kindly to criticism, having surrounded himself with a formidable clique of 'yes' men.

Oldham: "When we were having all the hits with the Small Faces, we weren't able to capitalise on it in the US. One hit in the US, then CBS pulled the plug and didn't promote *Ogdens'* because the Small Faces wouldn't tour. Anyway, it became apparent the CBS policy was recoup and bury. The CBS slogan for the time should have been, 'We want it and we'll bury it!' It was criminal."

Oldham and Calder took direct action: renting an apartment in the same residential block where Clive Davis lived, the ritzy Suite 24B, 80 Central Park West, overlooking Central Park.

Calder: "Clive rang up one morning and said, 'Have you got an appointment with me today at ten? Well meet me downstairs in 15 minutes, we'll go down to the office together'. So we get downstairs, and the bus comes along and we get on the bus and he puts the money in. We thought it was hysterical that he travelled to work on a bus. Clive got the record to No. 1 ['Itchycoo Park'] but he didn't bother to sell the album [*Ogdens'*]. I think Oldham upset him somehow. CBS were sitting on the records, still do it today. If a US record label decides to work the record they'll work the record. They can also go through the motions of making out they're working the record. If the president of the company doesn't call it a priority you're dead. You needed to know where their marketing was being spent, we didn't know at the time."

Lou Adler: "Oldham and I had similar situations at CBS. For me, it wasn't so much Clive Davis, it was the maze of departments and people you had to deal with. If you were like Oldham and myself, and were involved in all aspects of your artists' career and the records they made — producing, managing, art directing, marketing — you were naturally frustrated by the big company machine. I left CBS less than a year after making my deal."

The meeting between Davis, newly named CBS Vice-President Walter Yetnikoff, Oldham and Calder did not go well. The Immediate men were a good ten years younger than their CBS counterparts, far hipper and richer; a fact that seemed to irk the salaried company men. The four discussed Led Zeppelin, Oldham and Calder having been told by the group's founders, both Immediate stalwarts — Jimmy Page, who had recently left The Yardbirds, and John Paul Jones — that Led Zeppelin were available at $250,000 for a five-year deal. Calder and Oldham wanted the CBS men to put up half the cash and were flatly told they should be able to secure the deal themselves and, anyway, such a deal would not be valid because Page, as one of the Yardbirds — who had racked up four giant albums and several Top 20 singles in the US on the CBS owned Epic label — was still under contract to CBS.

This proved untrue, as no action was taken when Led Zeppelin signed to Atlantic at Page's asking price and would go on to be one of the biggest groups of 1969 in the US, their debut album selling over 700,000 copies.

Next Oldham and Calder brought up the débâcle of the Small Faces situation in the US. Davis and Yetnikoff had heard about the Fleetwood Mac fiasco. Calder was keen to talk about the British Blues albums. *Vol. 2* in the series had recently sold 18,406 in the US but many shops found it easier to get hold of the product straight from the UK and a further 5,000 albums had been sold on import.

The meeting soon degenerated and it was obvious to all that nothing productive would come of it. Later that day Oldham heard from Allen Klein. Davis had been on the phone: "Oldham and Immediate have no knowledge or understanding of the US market."

In frustration Oldham confronted Davis at his apartment later that day. It got heated and Oldham threatened to blow up the bus Davis travelled to work on. The CBS boss responded by having a restraining order issued, forbidding Oldham from going within a hundred feet of the CBS offices or his private residence. That was the end as far as Immediate were concerned.

The label's two-year distribution deal was due to expire in a few months and Oldham and Calder planned to keep on the New York apartment as a permanent base for Immediate operations in the US and attract new American distributors for the label and start afresh. Paul Banes was transferred from the UK to run the New York office. He had recently replaced Ken Mewis as Immediate Promotions Manager.

In US music trade magazine, *Record World*, under the headline, "Immediate Steps Up Stateside Activities", Banes said optimistically: "In England we have an identity and they tell us when we get it over here we'll really go places."

Banes: "I went into the office in London one morning, there was one stage where nobody knew what was going to be happening. Tony introduced me to Frank Chalmers who was our international person at EMI. I was going to be leaving and maybe going to work for EMI in France because it was a territory where EMI was not getting very far, our worst territory in Europe. I spoke to Frank about going to live in Paris, then suddenly out of the blue Tony said to me on Monday, 'Whattaya doing next week?' Basically I was off to [the US]. On the Saturday I had gone. They had found the apartment in New York, Jenny [Calder's wife] had already been out there buying furniture. She was there when I got there. We went to set up the office and everything outside of the UK was going to be routed through New York, all the royalties, all the statements, all the paperwork everything. I went out there and set up the bank accountants in New York, we set up two publishing companies, Nice Songs and Lovely Music and I was basically left to get on with it.

"Initially it was sorting out the paperwork. The CBS situation was unfortunate. We had done 400,000 with 'Itchycoo Park', but CBS couldn't follow it up. In the US there had been a big fuss because *Ogdens'* was in a round sleeve. There was bad blood over Led Zeppelin. It was all bollocks and it all got out of hand. If you look at the repertoire we took into CBS, what we had in the UK, what we put on the table, and us saying, 'We can get Led Zeppelin, all we need is

$150,000'. Then you get a fax back from Clive Davis saying Jimmy Page is under contract to us, which more or less means 'Fuck off'.

"Oldham had fallen out big style with Clive. We needed to do consistent sales in the US, that's where the money was. The company could have easily run on the back of what we were selling everywhere else. Andrew and Lou Adler met Clive Davis at Monterey Festival. Clive actually saw the two biggest producers either side of the water, Andrew with the Rolling Stones and Lou with the Mamas & the Papas and figures if he gets the two producers he gets the two acts. Unfortunately that didn't happen and CBS in New York was too fucking corporate. Dealing with them had been horrendous and we were all looking forward to the end of the deal with them and just moving on."

Instant

Oldham spent extended periods at the new Immediate offices in New York partying hard. There was cocaine and musicals *Hair* and *Oh! Calcutta!* to enjoy. He hit the town with pal Sean Kenny, occasionally Kenneth Tynan[97], the controversial Brit drama critic who had written *Oh! Calcutta!*, and a new brief best pal, movie star Richard Harris. The 37-year-old Irish actor had scored a huge screen hit with the musical *Camelot* and then taken the lengthy, melodramatic Jimmy Webb written 'MacArthur Park' to No. 1 on the US singles' chart. Harris had followed that up with 'The Yard Went On Forever', again written by Jimmy Webb, an anti-Vietnam song based on a speech by the late Robert Kennedy. Oldham enjoyed egging on Harris at various gigs on the actor's US concert tour.

Old friend Phil Spector was also up for a laugh again.

---

97. Kenneth Peacock Tynan (1927–1980) was an English theatre critic and writer who made his initial impact as a critic at *The Observer* in praise of John Osborne's *Look Back in Anger* (1956). In 1963, he was appointed as the new National Theatre Company's literary manager

An opponent of theatre censorship, Tynan is often believed to have been the first person to say "fuck" on British television, during a live broadcast in 1965, unfortunately no footage exists of this. However there have been at least three prior claims: Brendan Behan on *Panorama* in 1956 (although his drunken slurring was not understood); an anonymous man who painted the railings on Stranmillis Embankment alongside the River Lagan in Belfast in 1959 who told Ulster TV's magazine show, *Roundabout*, that his job was "fucking boring" and the actress Miriam Margolyes, who claims to have used the word in frustration whilst appearing on University Challenge in 1963.

It had been a few years now since his swansong with Ike and Tina Turner's 'River Deep, Mountain High' and he had recently signed a deal with A&M Records and come back strong with a Ronnettes single 'You Came, You Saw, You Conquered'. A lounge act he discovered while hanging out in Las Vegas, The Checkmates Ltd[98], had also been successful.

Another old pal, Kama Sutra's Art Kass[99], was in charge at the latest hot New York independent label, Buddah Records. Together with former Cameo Parkway player Neil Bogart (later famed for his Casablanca label), Kass was instigating a huge bubble-gum pop revival with Buddah. After all the serious heavy rock posturing at CBS, this really tickled Oldham.

Buddha had scored huge hits via production team Jerry Kasenetz and Jeff Katz. They were on a stupendous run and former Immediate recordee Joey Levine was the voice for a string of groups made up by the pair such as 1910 Fruitgum Company ['Simon Says', 'Chewy Chewy' and 'Yummy Yummy (Yummy I Got Love In My Tummy)']. While 'Sugar Sugar' by The Archies (the latest act from Monkees creator Don Kirshner) was another big bubble-gum hit at the time.

Immediate decided to go back to their roots — their

---

98. The group, discovered by Nancy Wilson, included both black and white members and had one major hit 'Black Pearl' (1969) produced by Spector. They broke up in 1970, but reunited in 1974 for a few more years and sang the national anthem for the *Thrilla in Manila* (Ali v Frazier II) in 1975.

99. Kama Sutra Records helped bolster MGM Records's profits during 1965 and 1966, primarily due to the success of The Lovin' Spoonful. Yet, dissatisfied with his distribution deal, Kass founded Buddah in 1967 to get out of the contract. One of his partners is alleged to have been Sonny Franzese (1917-2020), an underboss of the Colombo crime family who, it is said, used Buddha to launder illegal mob earnings.

love of the two-minute thrill — and attempted to set up a similar bubble-gum hit factory in London, creating a new imprint called Instant. Calder had argued against diluting the more mature image Immediate had garnered since delivering hit albums from the Small Faces, The Nice and with the Blues series.

Sean Kenny scribbled the Instant logo on a restaurant napkin and the sub-label was up and running, signing up writers such as Mike Finesilver and Peter Kerr[100], who had written and produced 'Fire' for The Crazy World Of Arthur Brown. Early releases on Instant included Oldham's production of Leeds outfit, The Outer Limits[101], who had previously recorded for Deram, with a sumptuously arranged, harmony-driven, pop sing-along 'Great Train Robbery', based on the Ronnie Biggs tale, written by the group's Jeff Christie. Finesilver and Kerr came up with a bouncing bit of London bubblegum, 'Happy Miranda' for the made-up group Excelsior Spring.

Twinkle[102] was Instant's star; a good-looking, hard-nosed 22-year-old Mod, she scored a UK hit with biker anthem 'Terry' and was one of a trio of Don Arden managed acts to record for the label. Twinkle wrote her

100. Born in Lossiemouth, Kerr escaped the Scottish civil service to become a professional jazz musician and appeared on bills featuring Shirley Bassey, Morecambe and Wise, Dusty Springfield and The Beatles before turning to freelance song-writing. In the 70s Peter returned to rural Scotland to become a farmer before moving to Spain where he became a best-selling travel writer.
101. The Outer Limits biggest hit came after they changed their name to Christie. Scoring a UK No. 1 (23 in the US) with 'Yellow River' and a No. 7 with 'San Bernadino' in 1970 before fading from view.
102. Lynn Annette Ripley (1948–2015), Twinkle owed her rapid entry into the recording studio at the age of 16 to her then-boyfriend Dec Cluskey, of The Bachelors. 'Terry' was a teenage tragedy song about the death of a boyfriend in a motorcycle crash which bore a resemblance to the Shangri-Las' 'Leader of the Pack'. The follow-up 'Golden Lights' was later covered by The Smiths.

own songs and Mike d'Abo was put to work producing her. They came up 'Soldier's Dream', but it was decided it would follow-up her debut 'Micky'. When 'Micky' was not a hit, 'Soldier's Dream' was shelved and Twinkle had a lost classic on her hands.

Arden's other two artists at Instant: Copperfield, with the bubble-gum-on-rote of 'Any Old Time (Your Lonely And Sad)' and a heavy rock album by Samson, *Are You Samson*, faired no better. The short-lived label's best-selling release was a football album, *Highlights of the 1968 European Cup Final* which was a recording of the BBC commentary of the Manchester United v Benfica match at Wembley (which United won to make them the first English club to win the European Cup). Oldham laughed when discussing *Highlights of the 1968 European Cup Final*, joking it featured an all-star line-up of Eusebio, Charlton and Best. The album also came in another *Ogdens'*-esque round sleeve, this time in the image of a football.

Instant also branched out into soundtracks, releasing the music from Peter Whitehead's new documentary film, *Tonite Lets All Make Love In London*, which had won acclaim at both the London and New York film festivals. The album featured the music of Pink Floyd, The Animals, Small Faces, Vashti, Twice As Much, Chris Farlowe and snippets of chat from Julie Christie, Lee Marvin, Mick Jagger, Michael Caine, Allan Ginsberg, David Hockney, Vanessa Redgrave and Edna O'Brien.

There were also plans for Instant to release the cast album for a new musical with which Oldham was involved. He had been spending relaxed afternoons in rehearsals at London's Mermaid Theatre with Sean Kenny at a production based on Jonathan Swift's *Gulliver's Travels*. Oldham was producing music for the show with d'Abo, who had also got the lead role in the production. D'Abo had won an Ivor Novello songwriting award for 'Build Me Up Buttercup' while still holding down his day job as singer in Manfred Mann. He was now being feted as "one of the first pop stars to cross over into theatre work".

Of his own move into theatre, Oldham told the *Daily Telegraph*: "At the moment I'm just amused by it, I don't know whether it's the novelty or not. There's a lot more bread in it than I actually thought. I originally started doing this just for fun."

D'Abo told the press: "Andrew encouraged me to be creative by producing and writing for Immediate. I had always felt awkward bringing my songs to the Manfreds but now I had free reign in my ideas. It was through my involvement with Immediate that Andrew set up a meeting with theatre director Sean Kenny. Bernard Miles [Mermaid Theatre's owner] had had a successful annual run with *Treasure Island* but for this particular Christmas they wanted to put on Sean's adaptation of *Gulliver's Travels* for the first time. I auditioned for the lead by reading the prologue and found they were already seriously considering me for the role. I was terribly excited."

Gulliver's Travels was a sell-out show and a single was planned for release — an Oldham produced, d'Abo-written song, '(See The Little People) Gulliver's Travels', on which the Small Faces had helped out in the studio. But Manfred Mann, having put up with d'Abo writing and producing for Immediate, objected to their singer fronting the single, essentially going solo. The band's leader, South African Manfred Mann[103], was "paranoid the single would be a hit

---

103. Born Manfred Sepse Lubowitz in Johannesburg (1940-), he was stongly opposed to apartheid and moved to the UK in 1961, writing in *Jazz News* under the pseudonym Manfred Manne (after jazz drummer Shelly Manne). The next year he met drummer and keyboard player Mike Hugg at Clacton Butlins Holiday Camp and formed a large blues-jazz band called the Mann-Hugg Blues Brothers which evolved into a five-piece group signing with EMI in 1963. The following year they turned to pop and scored the first of a string of hits with The Exciters' tune, 'Do Wah Diddy Diddy'.

and I would leave the group the same as [previous singer] Paul Jones had", d'Abo claimed.

"Our lawyers have told us not to comment," Calder told the press. In the end Mann successfully prevented d'Abo releasing the 'Gulliver's Travels' single and Oldham heavily remixed the entire soundtrack to the musical and released it as an Instant album. "I took it home and listened to it and thought, 'My God, what is this cacophony,'" said d'Abo. Oldham had cut up songs from the musical, looping and running them backwards over samples from The Lovin' Spoonful, Small Faces, The Nice, Little Richard and more. Soon after, d'Abo left both Immediate and Manfred Mann and would go on to star in the Broadway version of *Gulliver's Travels* with a new score written by Lionel Bart[104].

While Oldham indulged himself at the theatre, Calder followed a musical passion and hooked up with Maximum Sound studios and started a low-key rock steady and dub offshoot of Instant called Revolution. Singles were released from reggae star Owen Gray (who had previously cut for ska-friendly labels such as Bluebeat and Trojan) and Jimmy Scott, a Georgie Fame band member, who came up with 'Ob La Di Ob La Da Story', a notable adjunct to The Beatles hit. Paul McCartney explained: "I had a friend called Jimmy Scott who was a Nigerian conga player, a real cool guy. He had a few expressions, one of them was, 'Ob la di, ob la da, life goes on bra'. I said to him I really like that expression, and I'm thinking of using it, and I sent him a cheque in recognition of that fact later because, even

---

104. By this stage Bart's career was in steep decline. *Twang!!* (1965), a musical based on the Robin Hood legend, was a flop and *La Strada* (1969), which opened on Broadway after the removal of most of Bart's songs, closed after only one performance and by this time he was taking drugs and drinking heavily. He used his personal finances to try to rescue his last two productions, selling his past and future rights to *Oliver!* which he sold to entertainer Max Bygraves for £350 (Bygraves later sold them for £250,000).

though I had written the song and he didn't help me, it was his expression."

After these two singles, Revolution dovetailed with Instant to release a double a-side featuring reggae act Sonny Burke (who had recorded for Island, Bluebeat and Black Swan), and the Eddie Thornton Outfit (the brass section who had played on *Ogdens' Nut Gone Flake*) who were now working with Georgie Fame.

Calder also tried to sign The Equals to Instant. Featuring Eddy Grant, the band's UK No. 1 'Baby Come Back' was irresistible. The group's manager Eddie Kassner half-jokingly agreed to sell the band for "£25,000 cash in a brown paper bag" but when the cash was delivered, Kassner sent it back asking for double. The Equals stayed on President Records but Tony Calder would end up managing Grant in the 1980s during his second run at fame, including the era-defining singles 'Electric Avenue' and 'I Don't Wanna Dance'.

Instant product kept the staff at New Oxford Street busy while Immediate went through a fallow period. The Fleetwood Mac disaster had exposed how disinterested Oldham was, there had been no good news from the Small Faces for the longest time and The Nice were out of circulation, working on new material.

The company was now no longer the only maverick in town. The major labels all had their own "happening" imprints for new talent, such as Deram, Regal Zonophone and Polydor. There had also been a gallop from US labels to set up base in the UK (A&M, MCA and Warner Bros), and a swathe of young British entrepreneurs had been inspired by Immediate to try their own hand at creating something similar, such as The Who's Track records.

To cheekily remind the rest of the UK industry who was boss, Oldham and Calder pressed and packaged a 1968 UK album (200 copies) entitled the *Meditation Con*, and sent it to every managing director of every record and publishing company in the UK. It was their "comment on the state of the industry".

The album chronicled the following ruse: Oldham used unreleased Mamas & the Papas tapes, got Gered Mankowitz to take photos of eight 'hippie looking people' (the current vogue group look in the US) and sent a friend of his chauffeur Eddie round to new US label MCA, with the package, claiming to be the manager of the made-up band, now called The Gurus.

A series of meetings were held and taped between the Immediate stool and MCA head Mike Sloman. Oldham edited together snippets of the conversations. Sloman was caught declaring "people like me make important decision about what the public will or will not hear" and dishing out instructions to his secretary to "tell Mickie Most to fuck off".

Tony Calder: "We wired and taped everything. Sloman said the vocal harmonies in the mix weren't quite right, so could you get it re-done. The following week we sent the guy in with exactly the same acetate and Sloman said, 'Ah that's much better' and he agreed to sign them. That's when we had to call it off. But we released this 12" double-sided acetate and sent it to key people in the business. I think it destroyed Mike Sloman, which is quite sad, he was the head of MCA in the UK, and he died of pneumonia a few years later. But it started to show the hypocrisy of how the industry was working and that we weren't prepared to be hypocritical."

Paradise Lost

One morning Don Arden charged into the New Oxford Street offices wielding an axe and, once the laughter had subsided, was eager — as ever — to do business. After selling the Small Faces to Immediate, the fearsome rock impresario had built himself a useful stable of sixties stars notably Amen Corner who had scored major hits such as 'Bend Me, Shape Me' and 'High In The Sky' but Arden now wanted rid.

Don told me that he had arrived early to collect Amen Corner for a television recording and — finding them all out — and alarmed they'd miss the show – he broke in through the bedroom window of lead singer Andy Fairweather-Low. What he saw inside is one for the lawyers.

"At that stage," Arden told me, "I said, 'Go fuck yourself'. I just said 'Goodbye' and I did another sale. To me it meant nothing. My attitude was, 'Next please!' You didn't have to die for Amen Corner."

Arden had The Move as ready-made replacements and proposed Immediate take Amen Corner and their next single, '(If Paradise Is) Half As Nice'. He told Calder he could arrange for the group to switch from Decca-owned Deram to Immediate for £17,500. Calder wishfully telexed CBS to request $60,000 to sign the group and was turned down flat. He called Oldham to convince him 'Paradise' was a major hit in the making. "Is there enough money in the Immediate kitty to sign the group?" Oldham asked. Calder said not.

The cash was eventually put up out of Oldham's own pocket, supplied via Allen Klein — a forward against Oldham's Stones' earnings. Fairweather-Low recalled: "As

far as we knew we were managed by Ron King/Galaxy
Productions [a front for Arden]. Following the Hendrix
tour we turned up at the office to discover Arden sitting
in King's chair. He informed us we were now on the
Immediate label. It sounds strange but that's how it came
about, although it seemed cool to be on the same label as
Small Faces." Two weeks later, in early 1969, Immediate
released '(If Paradise Is) Half As Nice', produced by the
feted Kinks/Who producer Shel Talmy. The Immediate
advert for the single took up a whole front page of *NME*
and featured a starving African child with a begging bowl.

1968 had been a boon year for the UK record industry
with revenue topping £30 million. A hundred million
records had been sold, the highest number since 1964 when
singles accounted for the bulk of the sales. Now albums
accounted for that bulk and the singles market was soft.

From a dead start, 150,000 sales took '(If Paradise
Is) Half As Nice' straight to No. 1, replacing 'Blackberry
Way' by The Move. Calder had gambled by buying up vast
numbers illegally to get '(If Paradise Is) Half As Nice' to
No. 1 (a tactic he had also used to hype 'Man of the World'
up the charts), expecting to profit from the months of
continuous radio play and genuine sales that would follow.
And 'Paradise' did just that, slowly gliding on down over
11 weeks through the Top 40, selling 250,000 copies in the
UK.

Fairweather-Low told *NME*: "Immediate, our new
record label, are excellent at promoting groups. Look what
they have done for Small Faces and The Nice. Well maybe
The Nice's flag-burning thing was a mistake but we won't
go in for anything commercial like that."

Immediate swiftly followed the massive '(If Paradise Is)
Half As Nice' with 'Hello Susie', written by The Move's
Roy Wood. Produced again by Shel Talmy 'Hello Susie'
peaked at No.4.

Talmy: "I think I produced '(If Paradise Is) Half As

Nice' at Olympic Studios; good record, good band. Andy
Fairweather-Low certainly had a most unique voice. The
fact of the matter is I wanted a different record than 'Hello
Susie', which I think would have made them humongous
called 'At Last I've Got Somebody To Love' but Oldham
turned it down. They wanted 'Hello Susie'. I would feel a
lot better if someone paid me for them." It is thought that
Talmy never got paid at the time because Calder did not
like him — the same thing, incidentally, was said to have
happened to Duncan Browne.

'Hello Susie' was followed into the UK charts by Amen
Corner's debut album on Immediate, *The National Welsh
Coast Live Explosion Company*, recorded live at the Royal,
Tottenham. The album was a screaming teenybopper-fest
that featured covers of Lennon/McCartney's 'Penny Lane',
Jim Webb's 'MacArthur Park', and their previous big hit
singles 'Gin House', 'Bend Me, Shape Me', 'High In The
Sky' plus '(If Paradise Is) Half As Nice' and 'Hello Susie'.
Despite problems producing enough of the double album
sleeve jackets, *The National Welsh Coast Live Explosion Company*
made a decent showing in the UK Top 20.

Immediate promoted Amen Corner as the UK's most
"overground group". "Underground means a group with
a single that doesn't make the charts," Oldham told *NME*.
Privately, Oldham freely admitted Amen Corner did not
excite him. Aside from Fairweather-Low he couldn't name
another member of the group. "I went to see Amen Corner
live in Cardiff after the hit," he told me, "and thought to
myself, if this is show business what the fuck am I still doing
in here".

The issue over having to front the cash himself to sign
the group also brought home to Oldham how negligent
Immediate had become over finances. Over the years he
had constantly bailed out and propped up the label with
money from his Stones' earnings, the £25,000 he had
laid out to sign the Small Faces being the most substantial

amount. Now he knew he would soon be facing a large tax bill on all those earnings, a bill he was told was expected to be in the region of a half a million pounds. He warned Calder that from now the label had to be self-sufficient and the two agreed to downsize (much of the Immediate paperwork was now going through the new New York office anyway). New Oxford Street was closed and a new office: 111 Gloucester Place, W1, was being decorated. A US label starting up in London, Warner Bros, moving in to the old Immediate offices.

Calder's wife Jenny flew out to Paris to buy expensive chandeliers for the new gaff and Oldham splashed out to have the wife of his movie star friend Richard Harris acquire huge wooden church doors from the set of her husband's film *Camelot*, to separate his and Calder's new offices and these doors featured as backdrop to a group photo of all the Immediate staff and artists.

Another of Calder's cash-generating ideas involved holiday villas and a disco in Antigua, the popular Caribbean tourist destination with plans to launch a travel company called Instant Travel to take people to the upmarket enclave. He also oversaw re-releases of 'Hang On Sloopy', 'Out Of Time', and 'First Cut Is The Deepest' and a hastily hashed together Chris Farlowe compilation album made up of studio odds and ends, *The Last Goodbye*. There were also two more Blues albums, *The Beginning: British Blues* for the US market and a half-hearted *Blues Leftovers* for the UK market. None of these releases made much capital. Calder also over-estimated the longevity of Amen Corner as an act, especially in a climate where heavy rock dominated the more lucrative albums market.

Fairweather-Low (dubbed "one of Britain's most photographed and popular teenage faces") was asked by *Melody Maker*, "Did Andy — idol of the teenyboppers — feel the Amen Corner's scene was losing way to the underground groups? There had been many empty seats at Amen Corner's recent concert at the Royal Albert Hall's Pop Proms. Was it an indication that the nation's 'fave rave' group was beginning to wane?"

The group recorded a cover of The Beatles' No. 1 'Get Back' for a new single, yet despite another front-page *NME* Immediate advert to promote it, the Fairweather-Low produced track was a flop and, frustrated, he left the group[105].

"They have decided to abdicate their role as Britain's number one teenage group. The decision to disband was taken unanimously by the group at a time when they feel they have achieved all that is possible for them within the musically creative limitations of their particular markets," the group's new PR, former *NME* writer Keith Altham, told *Melody Maker*.

Immediate released an album *Farewell To The Real Magnificent Seven*, to 'commemorate' the Amen Corner split, featuring the group's three Immediate singles, with overblown adverts stating: "In 1936 Edward VIII abdicated his crown, his story is in words. In 1969 the Amen Corner abdicated their crown, this is their story in sound." The band said they came away from the Immediate deal with £2,000 split seven ways.

CBS were not interested in Amen Corner either. When '(If Paradise Is) Half As Nice' was at No. 1 in Europe, Allen Klein told Oldham that Clive Davis had told him that he did not believe the group were right for the market.

---

105. The group split in two with Fairweather Low leading Dennis Bryon (drums), Blue Weaver (organ), Clive Taylor (bass) and Neil Jones (guitar) into a new band, Fair Weather. They had a hit with 'Natural Sinner' (UK No. 6) in July 1970, but their subsequent albums failed to chart. Meanwhile saxophonist Allan Jones went on to form Judas Jump, a short-lived prog rock supergroup, that released one album and three singles before disbanding in 1971. Fairweather Low went on to a successful solo career in the 1970s, notably with the Top 10 hit 'Wide Eyed and Legless' (1975) and still tours today.

Paul Banes had eventually managed to get CBS to press '(If Paradise Is) Half As Nice' for US release but it sold just 1,904 copies. Then CBS, via their Epic imprint, released their own version of the song by the Dave Clark Five. An old record industry sage quietly informed Oldham, "You think you're very clever having got a 12 per cent record royalty from CBS but they only have to pay Dave Clark five per cent. So who do you think they're going to work?"

Calder next issued a "cool low-price" Immediate compilation album, *Immediate Lets You In*. This was pressed up in vast quantities and featured 'So Fine' by Amen Corner, 'Man Of The World' by Fleetwood Mac, 'Water On My Fire' by Albert Lee, 'Tribute To Elmore' by Eric Clapton and Jimmy Page, 'Hang On To A Dream' by The Nice, 'On Top Of The World' by John Mayall's Bluesbreakers and Eric Clapton, 'Recess' by Amen Corner and 'Lazy Sunday' by the Small Faces. The record sleeve featured snaps of the Immediate 'family' of artists montaged around a huge pair of smiling lips.

Calder also signed a new act, The Hill (a single 'Sylvie' was given limited release) and was in the process of completing the signing a new 'statement' artist for the label, the US singer Scott Walker[106]. Oldham was interested in this one. His friend Bob Crewe had written 'The Sun

---

106. Noel Scott Engel (1943-2019) was known for his emotive voice and the unorthodox stylistic path which took him from being a teen pop icon in the 1960s to an avant-garde musician in the 21st century. His first four solo albums reached the top ten in the UK where he lived from 1965, becoming a UK citizen in 1970.

He began a solo career with 1967's *Scott*, moving toward an increasingly challenging style. After sales of his solo work started to decrease he reunited with the Walker Brothers in the mid-70s but from the mid-80s onward Walker revived his solo career moving in an increasingly avant-garde direction. *The Guardian* described this transformation as "Andy Williams reinventing himself as Stockhausen". Walker continued to record until 2018.

Ain't Gonna Shine Anymore' for The Walker Brothers in 1965. Since then Walker, now a solo performer, had been turned on to the music of Jacques Brel by Oldham and Mort Shuman. He was managed by the gangster-linked Piccadilly records boss Maurice King (dubbed 'the monster' by Walker) and signed to the Philips label. King was interested in switching labels but asking a huge fee to breach the deal with Phillips that would then allow Walker free to sign with the label.

Calder was in negotiations but it was getting fractious. In the press, King[107] was blaming Immediate for Walker's failure to honour a fortnight club residency in Manchester and issued a writ against the label.

Tony Calder: "We had Scott Walker. He agreed. He was on board. He was going to record for Immediate. His manager tried to put injunctions on Oldham and me but in the end he gave up. Scott was ready to record. I negotiated the deal. I mean what a fucking star, but I couldn't deal with him. I was like, 'Andrew, you better get your arse over here fast, this guy's not in the real world'. Scott was talking about Brel, we were talking about Mort Shuman, he was talking about things I don't know about; he started talking about philosophy. I thought, 'What's this all about?' My idea of philosophy is a No. 1 hit record. I was out of my depth with Scott Walker. I just knew he could have been bigger than Frank Sinatra."

---

107. From *The Impossible Dream: The Story of Scott Walker and The Walker Brothers* by Anthony Reynolds. Tony Calder: "Maurice King came to see me one night with a gun. He said: 'You're not gonna take my boy! I'll shoot you!' I said: 'You're not gonna shoot me or else you would have done already!' "

Afterglow

Steve Marriott was a shared love that would briefly reignite and unite Oldham and Calder and galvanise Immediate. The label was desperate for the follow-up to the massive *Ogdens' Nut Gone Flake* but recording had ground to a halt as the group were stumped by how to progress past their "masterpiece". Marriott had caused much unrest in the studio and had more than once walked out on the group, notably after a New Year's Eve gig at Alexandra Palace. He'd also got a side project on the go with the 18-year-old Herd lead singer and "Face of 1968", Peter Frampton, who had played second guitar for the Small Faces at a few recent live shows. Marriott had produced a Frampton-written Herd single, 'Sunshine Cottage' for Deram records and wanted Frampton to become a permanent member of Small Faces. The rest of the group were against the move[108].

Marriott pressed ahead, rehearsing his side-project with

---

108. Frampton guested during a few of the Small Faces' live shows in October which, although well received by audiences, seemingly did nothing to convince Marriott's reluctant bandmates to allow Frampton to join them on a permanent basis. Consequently, Marriott was soon helping Frampton to form his own band as a backup plan.

In December 1968, at the behest of Glyn Johns, the Small Faces served as a backing band for French singer Johnny Hallyday during recording sessions in Paris for his latest album, *Rivière... Ouvre Ton lit* and Marriott invited Frampton along to participate. The week-long sessions may have been another of Marriott's attempts to test the waters to expand the Small Faces lineup, but tensions were reportedly brought to a head and the seeds sown for the group's break-up in the new year. The Hallyday sessions therefore proved to be the Small Faces' final studio recordings.

the aid of former Apostolic Intervention teen drummer Jerry Shirley, while playing on intermittently with the Small Faces. It proved impossible to keep these developments out of the press.

Immediate took out another front-page *NME* advert – titled 'The Anthology Of Speculation' — to advertise a surprise new single from the Small Faces, 'Afterglow (Of Your Love)'. The advert was a montage of music press news stories speculating on the future of the group, Marriott, Frampton and Immediate itself. Steve Marriott later said of the single: "It was Oldham's put together. By then I had already left Small Faces. The last complete thing we did together was the song 'The Autumn Stone', which was going to be the title track of the next Small Faces album, and 'Wham Bam Thank You Man'. Those two tracks were supposed to be a single but Oldham didn't like 'The Autumn Stone' and replaced it with 'Afterglow (Of Your Love)'. The irony is he wound up using 'The Autumn Stone' as a title for the album Immediate put out after we split. We had recorded a lot of tracks that we never had a chance to finish. They had titles just to mark the tape boxes, 'Colibosher', 'Wide Eyed Girl On The Wall', and they were thrown in as instrumentals. The three live tracks on *The Autumn Stone* were from Newcastle City Hall, just after *Ogdens'* came out. We had thought about a live album and wanted to see what it was like. At first Oldham wanted to use the stuff for Small Faces, who were going to continue without me, and Ronnie wanted me to help mix the stuff, so I did. There's probably more of it sitting around somewhere."

With no Small Faces to promote it, 'Afterglow (Of Your Love)' peaked at a disappointing No.36 in the UK with Marriott officially announcing his break from the group soon after: "My quitting is the best thing for them and for me. It will give both of us our freedom."

The lavishly packaged Small Faces double album, *The Autumn Stone*, which appeared soon after was, Oldham felt, a fitting tribute to the group's legacy, one he was proud to have been a part of, feeling their run on Immediate had been artistically and commercially satisfying for all concerned.

The truth was there was little mileage left in the group who had dropped off the pop radar since *Ogdens' Nut Gone Flake*, and had been left behind by the blues rock crowd and had never able to shake off their teenybopper following. The band's lack of success in the US had hurt most and in-fighting over the direction the band should take finally ripped them apart.

Oldham: "Tony Calder said to me one day, 'Pick a straw'. Then he explained we had a choice. We could either go with the three Faces — Kenney, Ronnie and Mac — wherever they were going to go with their lives or we could follow Stevie. I didn't regard it as a choice. Neither did Tony. Marriott was our man."

Immediate let one-time Cream road manager Billy Gaff take over the three remaining Small Faces. He put the Jeff Beck group guitarist Ronnie Wood and singer Rod Stewart in to replace Marriott and Small Faces became the Faces[109] and signed a lucrative deal with Warner Bros Records where they would go on and enjoy a new lease of life and fame.

Marriott christened his new outfit Humble Pie as Frampton quit The Herd. Their manager, Ken Howard, recalled: "We suddenly found the band's van in the street

---

109. The Faces had a unique arrangement, as Rod Stewart had signed a separate solo recording contract with Mercury shortly before joining the group, which was signed to Warner Bros. Band members often contributed to Stewart's solo albums as contract players, and Faces' live shows would feature as much of Stewart's solo material as that of the band. After the worldwide success of their third album, tensions came to a head during the recording of their fourth *Ooh La La* (1973). Lane left soon afterwards and Wood guested and then permanently joined the Stones in '76 just at the point when Stewart became a solo superstar in his own right.

outside the house: its tires had been let down. They said, 'We're going to Andrew Oldham'. What could one do? One couldn't sue them. It was particularly hurtful because we had a No.2 record and had notched up three hits with the group. They were poised for very big things. We just thought, 'Why?'"

Under Howard and co-manager, Ken Blakely, The Herd had been pop fodder featured heavily in magazines aimed at teenage girls and had scored Top 20 hits with 'Paradise Lost' and 'From The Underworld' in 1967 and had gone Top 5 with 'I Don't Want Our Loving To Die' in 1968. The Herd's producer, Steve Rowland, was more tenacious than the band's managers. He claimed Frampton was under worldwide contract to his Double R Productions until 1971 and fought hard to protect his interest. The legal wrangling took weeks, with Immediate eventually admitting defeat and paying what was reported to be $24,000 to lift the injunction. Oldham was forced to admit defeat on this one and fronted the money from his own pocket, eager to get Marriott's new group off the ground.

After the expensively delayed start a front-page story in *Melody Maker* welcomed Humble Pie as a "Pop Giant's Supergroup", and told how "two of Britain's biggest pop idols", Marriott and Frampton, had been secretly rehearsing for weeks with Jerry Shirley and bassist Greg Ridley.

Immediate took out an advert that spanned the front and back page of *NME* making an A2-size poster of a David Bailey photograph of the four Humble Pie musicians, to promote the group's debut single, 'Natural Born Bugie'. The advert was part of a mammoth press promotion, the label's biggest ever, with more full page adverts in *Record Retailer, Rolling Stone, International Times, Oz, Black Dwarf* and *Time Out*, as well as special posters and window displays for the 140 shops in the WH Smiths chain.

The first 50,000 copies of 'Natural Born Bugie', written by Marriott but sung by Frampton, were encased in an expensive colour sleeve featuring another David Bailey photograph of the group. Humble Pie's debut album, *As Safe As Yesterday Is*, was in the can and Immediate promised "the most complete packaging concept ever" for its release.

Humble Pie debuted live at Ronnie Scott's jazz club and in press interviews Marriott said: "I've never been so excited about anything as I am about the group. We're going to be a heavy music band." Still only 22, Marriott was careering from Mod to rocker, hoping, he said, to avoid the "old pop star bit" with his new group. "The single doesn't lay any schmaltz," he told one interviewer. Prompted by accusations that it sounded pretty close to The Beatles track 'Get Back', he explained: "It's a bit like 'It's Not Easy' [from the Stones' *Aftermath* album], with a sound like the Bill Black Combo."

When the group performed the single on *Top of the Pops* Frampton said he was just glad he didn't have to spend two hours in the make-up room and then forced to have eye-drops that would make it look as though he was about to cry, the way he had been for previous appearances with The Herd.

Jerry Shirley: "Once Oldham got wind of the fact that we were gonna get Humble Pie together he came up and stood at the plate. There were other managers at the time and other record labels interested, but Oldham just came up and said, 'I'll do this, however you wanna do it, whenever you wanna do it, let's go to bat'. He had this remarkable knack of spotting a hit single. We recorded this little song that was a Chuck Berry rip-off that was called 'Natural Born Bugie'. The term 'bugie' back then was considered derogatory because it had the same kinda connotation as the word 'nigger' today. We had no idea; we thought it was like boogie-woogie. The song was a throwaway that Steve had come up with a direct rip-off from 'Little Queenie'. Oldham came into the studio and said, 'That's the single'. We said no but within five or six weeks it was No. 1 across

Europe.

"Steve had been very much the front man in Small Faces but when it came to Humble Pie in the early days it was much more Peter Frampton's band. Steve just wanted to relax and groove. It was Peter and I that put the band together. I got in because Peter wanted a drummer that sounded like Kenney Jones. Really Steve just wanted to kick back and play a little guitar and not be the manic front man, that's really where he was at in the beginning. He wanted to see Greg Ridley and Peter shine more than himself, and then it all changed because Steve just had this very powerful presence on stage and after a while, as Humble Pie went on, he was being encouraged by all those around us, management wise, to take the forefront. Anyway, it was his natural way to do that."

'Natural Born Bugie' reached No.4 in the UK with ten weeks of strong sales to come and made No. 1 in Holland, Belgium and Germany. Immediate dressed the Pie's debut album, *As Safe As Yesterday Is*, to look as if it were a parcel wrapped in brown packing paper, tied by string, with the album information as the address and the photos of the band by David Bailey tucked away as mock postage stamps.

Produced at Olympic Studios by Andy Johns, the brother of Stones' engineer Glyn Johns, this was the other half of Marriott's moon. He shared co-writing credits with Frampton on the album's title track and had written the lion's share of the rest of the album. "We've done our second album already and it has got a beautiful sound," Marriott said unhelpfully during press interviews

Marriott recalled: "My missus helped me with the whole changeover scene. You need someone who can give you advice and understands. If Humble Pie hadn't happened, I would have stayed on in the Small Faces, bringing everybody down. I never ever thought I would leave the Small Faces. I thought it would just go on forever. But it feels like Humble Pie has been together for years. I just want to be part of the band and do my job. I don't have to freak out anymore. I can relax and play music."

Special displays and posters were distributed to all the record dealers in the UK, but after a good first week, in at No.15 in the *Record Retailer* charts, sales for *As Safe As Yesterday Is* dropped off, with many questioning why the hit single was not included on the album — a practice, Oldham wryly reflected, that had once endeared the Stones to the public.

Marriott was keen to tour and took Humble Pie on the road in Europe. Amsterdam's The Paradise Club became the band's main base of operations as they hit the European promo and festival circuit in Italy, Switzerland, Belgium, and Germany.

During the long delay in launching the group, Humble Pie had, as Marriott said, recorded their second album and Immediate rushed to release it. *Town and Country* showed a lighter, more acoustic and country-tinged, sound than on their earthy rock debut. "A little more contrived but a lot more relaxed," said Marriott in interviews.

He added: "There's more clarity on it than the first. People criticised us for being muzzy but it was meant to be that way because it was like a live thing. There's more recording technique on the second. The first was not representative of what we are doing now. I am really pleased with the second album much more than the first."

The album, again produced by Andy Johns at Olympic studios, had a couple of potential singles: Marriott's take on Buddy Holly's 'Heartbeat' and his own song 'Down Home Again' but Immediate plumped for 'The Sad Bag Of Shaky Jake' with promo copies sent out to record stations as the band embarked on their debut UK tour, a package called *Changes 1969*, which was advertised via an *NME* front cover. Humble Pie were supported by David Bowie, who was scoring with his first hit, 'Space Oddity'. The stage show, designed by Sean Kenny, stopped in at venues such as the Queen Elizabeth Hall at the Southbank Centre in London.

Jerry Shirley: "Sean Kenny came up with a bizarre set that had this huge white elephant with smoke blowing out of its ass. Oldham was very committed to being on the road with us. The other bands on Immediate he was bored with or weren't pulling his chain. He gave us that great big Rolls Royce to travel England in with Eddie driving. That was our tour vehicle. In the UK on the tour with David Bowie we were still doing a lot of the acoustic stuff as a reaction to all that supergroup publicity. We were trying to say, don't expect too much, give us a chance to grow, we haven't found our niche yet. It was going to America that made us realise we had to get down and do some serious rock and rolling."

Humble Pie

Humble Pie headed to the US full of great hope. Post-Woodstock, hairy, heavy, bluesy album rock with a country twinge dominated the airwaves and there were many UK acts cashing in big time. The Stones had returned as popular as ever, Led Zeppelin were going down a storm and Blind Faith (another 'supergroup', made up of Cream's Eric Clapton, Ginger Baker and Traffic vocalist Steve Winwood) had been commanding up to $25,000 per concert.

They arrived for a six-week US college tour in June 1969 – the first time the US got a taste of Marriott in the flesh. Immediate's two-year US distribution deal with CBS had expired and Oldham and Calder began to attract new US bidders for the group and/or the label. Oldham was buoyed with thoughts of getting a clean crack at the US with Humble Pie. There was, however, a clause in the original Immediate/CBS contract that allowed CBS a third-year option on US rights for Immediate product. But as the first two-year period had been so marked by failure and antagonism, it was a taken as given CBS would not extend the contract. When CBS President Clive Davis, handed Immediate's US office manager, Paul Banes, a cheque for $50,000 and another $6,000 for royalties owed to Immediate, and informed him CBS were going to take up that third-year option, it was the beginning of the end.

It was at this point that Oldham filed his $7 million lawsuit claiming CBS had repeatedly breached its obligations and that the third-year option was unenforceable. He said that CBS and the defendant, Clive Davis "wilfully and maliciously purported to exercise the option to extend the agreement for another year (to 31 July, 1970), not for the purpose of distributing Immediate records, but to suppress Immediate as a competitor in the US and Canada, and to injure the plaintiffs financially".

Oldham continued: "The CBS relationship with Immediate had been, almost consistently, one of market foreclosure, arbitrary refusal to distribute and wanton disregard for principles of fair dealing".

He repeated Clive Davis' words as told to Klein that "Immediate did not know anything about the US market" and that Immediate artists were not the right type to have alongside his new CBS signings as they did not "fit into his ideal".

Explaining the situation to me, Oldham compared the way CBS treated Immediate to the way UK record companies between 1955–1964 had treated US labels — paying large advances for the US product, and then burying it while they recorded and promoted their own cover versions for a bigger return.

CBS, Oldham maintained, had "destroyed" Immediate in the US. Figures were compiled that showed comparative sales of Immediate records in the US and the UK, from 1 August 1967 (the start date of the CBS agreement), to 1969. In the US there had been approximately 375,759 singles and 159,990 albums sold, while during the same period, EMI distribution of these records resulted in sales of close to a million singles and 500,000 albums. "This", Oldham pointed out "despite the UK accounting for only six to ten per cent of the world market for records, as compared with the US which accounts for 50 per cent".

Oldham: "On or about 11 April, 1969, I engaged the defendant, Clive Davis, in a lengthy telephone conversation regarding Immediate's and my own dissatisfaction with CBS's efforts on our behalf. The gist of my remarks were that Immediate had suffered long enough at CBS's hands and that the agreement had been breached so many times by CBS that it was effectively of no force and that Immediate should be free to secure adequate distribution of its records in the US and Canada from other sources.

"Davis, after substantial personal abuse of me and other Immediate employees, stated that, 'To teach us a lesson' CBS would exercise its option to extend the agreement for an additional year and during that period would do nothing with the records. Davis said, 'We've got you the way we want you and we'll keep you there and we'll tie you up for another year' and he did not wish to speak to me or hear from me, or anyone from Immediate."

Davis employed a team of top New York lawyers to pick through Oldham's Affidavit, creating a seemingly never-ending paper trail. Davis, now the most celebrated record exec in American music biz history, has a chequered history and reputation. While I worked on Oldham's memoirs I got in touch with him and he sent a fax back which said: "Andrew Oldham was always at or near the cutting edge. He was very informed and professional, always receptive and responsive. We enjoyably shared much success."

Immediate issued a statement to the US press to declare they were going independent in the US, disassociating themselves completely from CBS. In the statement they admitted that "innovating a new direct distribution plan in the US" was a major change for the company and "as of the moment, pressing, distributing and promotion policies have not been finalised".

The statement concluded: "This policy has been adopted after careful consideration by Immediate as the only method of servicing, distributing and promoting our product in the US to gain the same efficiency, total responsibility and complete involvement that we feel our product deserves. The label will continue to be distributed throughout the rest of the world by EMI and independent US release dates are scheduled for Humble Pie and The Nice."

Tony Calder: "We had no alternative but to go independent. We were no longer welcome at CBS and Oldham had made sure that we weren't welcome at any other [US] record companies because by then these executives didn't want to be told they were arseholes. It was a very brave move to make at the time, even today there's no such thing as a successful UK independent set up in the same way in the US."

Paul Banes: "Overnight, Oldham came in and said, 'We're doing it ourselves, get on the phone'. We got on the phone and called all these independent distributors. Oldham took out this amazing, quadruple-page spread for Humble Pie in *Billboard*, fucking unreal, the label looked great, the whole thing. I went on the road with Humble Pie, did the whole tour, going back to the office in New York when I could. Six and a half weeks on the road with Humble Pie wasn't the easiest thing in the world as we were working on $8 each per day. Oldham came to New York with Steve Inglis and Sean Kenny. I picked them up at the airport. Oldham had this concoction he would drink that was *consommé* and vodka. He would get out a tin of soup, heat it up, fill up the tin with vodka, tip that in and then we would go out."

Setting up as an independent in the US cost Immediate close to $50,000. Over the course of a few weeks Paul Banes arranged for RCA's pressing plant to make up 40,000 copies of Humble Pie's *As Safe As Yesterday Is* and 25,000 of the group's (re-named for the US) debut single, 'Natural Born Woman'.

An ordeal for Banes was getting the backing of US independent distributors but agreements were eventually drawn up with ten of the biggest and most powerful in the US, including Universal Schwartz in Philadelphia, guaranteeing the label coast-to-coast distribution. Although each of the new US distributors had their own promotion men — in order to guarantee the fullest coverage for Immediate product — five independent promotion men were hired at $2,000 a month. Banes also collected a complete dossier on US radio stations, DJs, trade publications and underground magazines and he and Oldham spent an afternoon visiting the key radio stations in New York.

There was a $15,000 budget for advertising Humble Pie in the US with glossy foldout adverts featuring in *Cashbox* and *Record World*.

Oldham, reflecting on these weeks, funding all this from his own pocket, suggested to me that he must have been "befuddled by drugs and drink", acting out of wounded pride more than anything. He gave several interviews about Immediate's new position in the US press under headlines such as "Immediate To Go Direct in US" and "Immediate Goes Indie". Oldham told *Cashbox*: "All acts on the label are self-contained. They write their own material and produce themselves."

Advance copies of 'Natural Born Woman' started to receive airplay throughout the US and made the "up and coming" chart of *Record World*.

As Safe As Yesterday Is was also picking up glowing reviews in the US press. *Billboard* praised "a strong commercial package and underground-orientated numbers". *Record World* called the album: "Head-turning rock and roll, a very powerful smile, moving from heavy rock to country funk to poetic folk-jazz, Humble Pie display considerable talent and energy. Keep tabs on this set, they could be big."

A Pie show at the packed Fillmore East in New York, supporting Butterfield Blues Band and Santana, was "considered one of the happiest pop events of 1969" by *Cashbox*. "Humble Pie are well on their way to innovative rock stardom," reckoned the influential weekly. The review went on: "The act begins quietly with a solo song by Pete accompanying himself on acoustic guitar. Greg Ridley then sings his solo with Pete joining him as second guitarist.

The non-electric segment ends with Steve singing lead on a Scottish folk song done in three-part harmony. A quick switch to amplification and the group is off on an extended jam of Dr John material, 'Walk On Gilded Splinters' and 'Gris Gris Gumbo Ya Ya'. Humble Pie's presentation is much like Crosby, Stills, et al's, in that they both feature beautiful and intricate vocals in which different people take over lead. The music moved from country to blues to real jazz and on to straight rock with an enviable fluidity. And Stevie's guitar work was frighteningly good (frightening because very few people in this country have heard of him). Given six months, with a national tour under its belt, Humble Pie will return to the Fillmore topping the bill."

Oldham flew in and out of the Humble Pie tour, partying hard and cutting a live album; recorded in LA at Whiskey A-Go-Go, as the band rocked out on covers such as: The Yardbirds 'For Your Love', Johnnie Kidd and The Pirates' 'Shakin' All Over' and Ray Charles/Eddie Cochran's 'Hallelujah, I Love Her'.

Oldham based himself at the weekend home of Dan Crewe, the brother and business partner of US record producer and songwriter Bob Crewe. It was within easy commuting distance of New York, in countrified Connecticut, a classic New England five-bedroom, swimming pooled mansion, set in eight acres of land. Humble Pie and various UK acts such as Joe Cocker would drop by between gigs to party.

Dan Crewe: "In California, Humble Pie were appearing at Whiskey A-Go-Go and Oldham was recording them for a live album. He was in the control booth and he overdosed and passed out on the control panel. He was literally dead meat, I was scared to death, I thought he was gonna die on me. I spent the next two hours with him traipsed around my shoulders walking up and down Sunset Boulevard, trying to keep him alive. Later that night Whiskey A-Go-Go burnt down. Everyone knew Oldham by this point, they knew what a problem he was and he was a *big* problem. He was getting antagonistic in social situations, very apt to throwing tantrums and getting into fights. It was not the kind of thing you would eagerly get involved in.

"There was a lot of talk about CBS having attempted to destroy Immediate, both Oldham and Tony had the feeling that there was a plot to bury the label. By this time Oldham had become pretty damned outrageous and arrogant and would say some terrible things to people, he was no longer being very political. Clive Davis is the kind of person to say, very quietly, 'Kill 'em, make the label go away'. Why else would a company that had the rights to somebody who had a track record of making very substantial hits be buried? Either they weren't producing records that were right for the market or CBS was going out of their way to snuff them out."

The Nice's manager, Tony Stratton-Smith, was outraged and confused by Immediate's new independent status in the US. In the UK the group's third Immediate album, *Nice*, proved what a significant act they were becoming, debuting at No.3 in the UK charts.

Immediate coupled a poppy take on the Tim Hardin song 'Hang On To A Dream' with 'Diary Of An Empty Dream' for a single. A head-in-the-oven suicide picture was featured on the sleeve. The group wanted to hire a 60-piece symphony orchestra for a couple of showcase dates in New York and LA. Immediate sounded out Joseph Eger, conductor of the New York Symphony Orchestra, and discovered his fees would be astronomical.

The Nice (without orchestra) played headline gigs at New York's Fillmore East and with Eric Clapton and his current rave, Delaney and Bonnie[110], at Philadelphia's

---

110. Singer-songwriters Delaney and Bonnie Bramlett fronted a rock/

Electric Factory. Paul Banes organised television shows and various radio promo spots for the group and Immediate redesigned and re-titled the *Nice* album for release in the US and independently pressed up 250,000 of the album, *Everything As Nice As Mother Makes It*, expecting to do some serious progressive rock business.

CBS objected; raised an injunction and prevented the release of the album, threatening legal action against Immediate's independent distributors. The label then pressed up 250,000 copies of the same album at their own plants and charged it to the Immediate account.

Stratton-Smith remembers: "My last meeting with Oldham was at the Speakeasy when we threatened to have a punch up as a result of the way he was failing to give any support, when the Nice badly needed it in. We were stuck with Oldham at a time when he was distributed by CBS but at Clive Davis' personal instruction, he was not allowed to enter the CBS building. So it was very amusing to be with a record company that was itself on an answering machine in a Central Park apartment. Nor could we go to CBS because officially we weren't their artists, we were Andrew Oldham's artists. We couldn't get any action on the records. It was very frustrating."

Oldham told me that this was what Stratton-Smith had spent "every waking hour of his miserable life waiting for", trying to break The Nice contract so he could jump-start his own record label, Charisma. Stratton-Smith used the chaos in the US to cut all ties with Immediate, took with

---

soul ensemble whose members at different times included Duane and Gregg Allman, George Harrison and Leon Russell to name just a few. Delaney had been a session musician, Bonnie was the first white Ikette in the Ike & Tina Revue. They married in 1967. After a successful album, *On Tour With Eric Clapton*, by late 1971 their marriage showed signs of strain. Bonnie later described their relationship as abusive due to their cocaine addictions, and they fought often. They divorced in 1972.

him an album in the can that Immediate had paid for and put it out in his own Charisma[111] Records in the UK.

Paul Banes: "Tony Stratton-Smith, although he may be dead, was a shit-faced little git who stole our fucking tapes. The Nice live tapes we recorded in the US for the album after *Everything As Nice As Mother Makes It* cost us £2,500. Andrew paid for it out of his own pocket. Stratton-Smith went into the studio in London, where the LP was being mixed, paid the bill, walked out with the tapes and set up Charisma Records on the back of that. That LP did 170,000, it was the biggest album The Nice had, it was what we had been working toward all the time, because the whole thing with The Nice was to see them live. They got an album that cost them fuck all and it cost us heavy grief. CBS were saying, 'Immediate acts belong to us'. We were saying, 'No they don't because you haven't done anything for our records. The fact that you haven't put them out is a restrictive trade thing'. We went to court with the Kennedy lawyers."

---

111. Charisma went on to record some of the biggest acts of the next decade, including Lindisfarne, Hawkwind, Van Der Graaf Generator, Genesis and Peter Gabriel before being bought by Virgin in 1983.

Drugs, Drugs and More Drugs

Dan Crewe flew back to London with Oldham to try and, he said, help the man as much as Immediate. He went through the finances of both. Immediate was a mess and one particular entry in the books deeply troubled Crewe.

Here we go: a final twist. Ironic really. Immediate had recently paid US major label United Artists $50,000 as part of a legal settlement regarding a 1967 deal which had gone badly wrong. It's difficult to know who to blame: Laurel or Hardy. It happened when Oldham was making the distribution arrangement with CBS. At the same time, United Artists paid Calder a $50,000 advance for the same rights. To set Immediate free to sign with CBS, United Artists had demanded a whopping $225,000 to terminate and void their contract. The payments had been staggered: $25,000 of the debt had been paid back in 1968, the $50,000 was 1969's payment and the final $175,000 was due in 1970.

Tony Calder: "Andrew was at one of the sleep treatment centres in London, the Bethanie Nursing Home. It didn't bother me. You never knew if it was him or the drugs talking. A pal of mine, Martin Davis from United Artists, called and said, 'Do you wanna make a deal for Immediate in America?' The deal was done in three days. They paid the money, $50,000, and they were gonna put the records out. Then Andrew came out of the Bethanie and started screaming, 'Fuck United Artists!' and flew off to see Lou Adler in LA for Monterey, bumped into Clive Davis and did the deal for Immediate with CBS without even speaking to me. CBS, he said, was the ultimate record company in the US; Lou was dealing with them, they had Janis Joplin. I was calling him at the Bethanie Nursing Home. I said, 'Could I speak with Mr Oldham?' They said, 'He's asleep and he'll be asleep for another week'. How can you do business like that? I went back to United Artists and asked to get out of the deal. Sid Shemmel was their lawyer; the boss of United Artists in the US was this huge overweight guy, Mike Stewart. I heard him say, 'Screw the bastards' to Sid Shemmel."

"Our legal counsel was drugs, drugs and more drugs," Oldham told me.

Crewe discovered Oldham's private financial affairs were also in disarray, with overdue demands for a personal UK tax bill of approximately £600,000 (part of the same Inland Revenue effort that would drive the Stones to leave England to take up residence overseas).

Dan Crewe: "They had committed to paying a lot of money to United Artists on the debenture and they thought rather blithely that this would be no problem, all they would have to do was have a couple of hit records. Immediate was living way beyond its means, living as if it was always gonna be successful. Neither Andrew Oldham nor Tony Calder thought of the consequences of over-commitment without having the resources. The people who run the company ultimately have to take the responsibility. This is where the drugs start to cloud your thinking. You think that if we do something that's very grand, people will think we are successful and therefore we will be successful. There was more hype than reality.

"There was little or no money and there was a lifestyle that nobody wanted to put a stop to. Andrew and Tony caught the crest of a wave and rode it. They never realised when the wave was over, and in order to sustain themselves, they had to rethink the process, reinvent themselves. They could not sustain themselves in this kind of childish, 'We are indestructible' mentality. [The company philosophy was] 'Everybody else are fools, all the record people, they're all fools, all the important people in the industry, they're fools.' The proof of the pudding is no-one is that special unless you're really watching what you're doing.

"Oldham was in a state. I advised him to close Immediate down, it was a farce, and Oldham would be much better off making a deal for the artists directly with a label, letting them take responsibility for the overhead. If there was gonna be any success at all, stick with what you know best, produce and promote. I never had great overwhelming respect for Tony, I don't know what he was doing, he was supposed to be the business head of the company, he was supposed to control it and he wasn't. So in the long run he was never an asset. Oldham had a partner who was not doing what he had to, even if that meant saying, 'I can't do this, I'm out of here'. Instead, he was virtually doing the same things as Oldham. It was self-delusional.

"Oldham hadn't got the message yet about what he had to do for himself. He didn't realise that his problems lay within himself. He had become a drug addict and an alcoholic. He operated every waking hour in a constant state of drug addiction, alcohol or both. I spent my time mostly looking at how to salvage Oldham. That was my focus. Oldham had every bank on the phone. I was amazed at the tolerance of the banks and why they hadn't foreclosed on him. I would go in and talk to the banks but it was really like sticking your finger in a dyke. There were leaks everywhere. It was just horrific.

"Oldham was out of his mind as far as using, and he had this constant conflict with his then wife. It's hard to lay the blame in any one place in a case like that, there was enough blame for everybody and Oldham did nothing to help the situation. It was awful to come over there and give him nothing but bad news. He owed everybody; he had a high overhead, he had mortgages, he had loans, and he had overdrafts. Oh God, what a mess.

"I advised him to put the label in to liquidation mainly

to protect himself. The truth of the matter is he came out of it by the skin of his teeth. He didn't come out of it clean with everything intact. He came out of it with not having to be a bankrupt — but just barely. He would be on drugs where he couldn't talk, his mouth would just go to mush and he would drink on it."

Ken East, Managing Director of EMI: "Andrew came in one day to EMI; he was getting into trouble and we could see he was. EMI were fairly safe because if we didn't sell the records they were his, we manufactured them at his expense. But it was of no interest to us for him to get into trouble because it's good business being lost. He was very independent, you couldn't tell him anything because he knew it all, likewise Tony Calder.

"Oldham was never a dishonest person, just nutty that's all. I never worked out the relationship with Tony Calder, whether it was a love-hate relationship or whether Tony tended to push Oldham into areas he couldn't get out of. When you got the two of them together it was like an act, on their own they were different people. You could sit down and talk more sensibly with Tony but things would never really turn out the way they should turn out. With Oldham you couldn't agree on anything because he never had the ability or the mood to talk business in any way. He was just so up in the air about everything. Other people that had to deal with him at EMI, and I don't blame them, would say, 'Oh Christ is it worth it, the aggro that this fella creates for us?' Most of these people were in sales, and they were the most affected by the things he did. But, of course, it was worth it because we had got a business and he was selling a lot of records. Indirectly that reflected on the credibility of EMI. We performed properly for Oldham, which wasn't always the easiest thing to do. There was no way EMI could keep Immediate going, it was beyond repair, they were still running around Europe buying doors for elaborate offices."

Tony Calder: "By the end of the 1960s when we should

have had major success in the US, there were now coming in rules and regulations; there were certain people's arses you had to kiss. Whereas before people were kissing our arse. Oldham didn't want to kiss arse. I wasn't concerned about Oldham's mental state; my main concern was trying to keep the company going. We nearly merged with Chris Blackwell at Island, we sold singles, and he sold albums. We had a meeting, we were gonna put the two companies together and it all fell apart when Oldham came out of the clinic and met with Blackwell. Then it was all off. I don't think Blackwell liked the state he was in. Then when I got my stomach ulcer I just snapped. Oldham's efforts were totally destructive to the point where one of us had to go."

Freddie Bienstock, owner of Carlin Music: "When it looked as if Immediate was going to collapse, Tony Calder came to see me and tried to arrange a deal, telling me how well the company was doing. In the afternoon Oldham came over and I said to him, 'Listen, Tony Calder was painting a rather optimistic picture about the prospects of the company'. Oldham told me, 'Don't believe a word he says, it's all bullshit'.

"Oldham was living in this big house in Richmond and he hadn't paid his grocer's bills for the longest time, he owed over £200. I happened to be visiting when the grocer appeared to collect his money. Oldham let him in and gave him a joint. Two hours later this grocer was bumped out of his head, the happiest grocer you ever saw, he never got a penny but he was in great shape. Oldham told me that should the police come to his house he had a secret passage that went underground that he could get through and out somewhere. Oldham made a lot of money and blew a lot in the craziest way, and Tony Calder was quite some help in that."

Paul Banes: "It was five days before Christmas 1970. I got back to the office in New York and Oldham and Tony are in the middle of a discussion. They tell me to go and take a walk. I went out and when I came back, Tony says, 'We've broken up, I'm leaving and going to Antigua'. I was sitting in New York holding the baby and we've got a song called 'Going Home' by Ten Years After, a track Immediate Music had an interest in, on the Woodstock album. We had 15 minutes; it was worth £1 million. Anybody with the right attitude would have known what we already knew about the Woodstock album. The only person who didn't was Danny Crewe."

Tony Calder: "I was haemorrhaging, walking around bleeding. Andrew bought me out neatly within 24 hours, it was 30 December 1969, it was done privately, the money didn't come out of Immediate, it all came out of his Rolling Stones income."

Malcolm Forrester, Head of Immediate Music: "Tony bottled out. He wasn't there. There was a handwritten letter from him on aeroplane paper, advising Oldham what to do to save the company. It was almost unintelligible. We were told Calder was getting bruises all over his body, we actually thought he was really ill. When he and Oldham fell out the staff had split into two camps, there was a really bad atmosphere. We purchased accountants and lawyers, in London and New York, as if they were going out of fashion. I'd fallen in behind Tony, you never saw Oldham in the office. The move from New Oxford Street to Gloucester Place was not a good move. We were always leasing premises when we could have bought them. When Calder went to Antigua I started working more closely with Oldham."

Calder was bought out for around £26,000, plus a UK house and the house in Antigua, a claimed salary, a Mercedes 600 (eventually sold to Pete Townshend) and forgiveness of monies owed. Oldham, still just 26, was living alone in the penthouse above the now deserted Immediate Gloucester Place offices, clinging on to the last vestiges of power. Every night he would leave a note out at night for his butler Ted, a retired sailor, telling him what he wanted for breakfast and what record he required to be woken up with.

Mario and Franco at the Trattoria Terrazzo restaurant in Soho insisted, after all the good years, Oldham eat for free and there was a steady supply of the mood elevator Ritalin to stop him wallowing in the badness of his private and professional life. To handle the Immediate liquidation he hired a top London accountancy firm, Stoy Hayward, experts in insolvency work. The creditors' meeting was held at the firm's Wigmore Street offices.

Oldham: "On the day of the creditors meeting Dr Robertson did his job, I was pretty calm and couldn't be bothered to hit anyone. He even helped me sort out what to wear, a purple velvet jacket and grey flannel trousers, advising against a suit as that spelt money to the vultures."

Martin Spenser, Specialist in Liquidation and Receiverships at Stoy Hayward: "Oldham was the largest creditor, all told he had sunk about a quarter of a million pounds into it. The outside creditors were relatively small. In a normal case if you have a company that is liquidated and there are, say, 100 creditors on the statement of affairs, you can expect that roughly ten per cent of the creditors will turn up. With the Immediate liquidation, the receptionist rang me up about half an hour before the meeting, quite frantic to say that there were over 100 people milling about in the reception. When the meeting started, there was an overflow of another 80 people outside the boardroom and the impression I got was that most of them weren't creditors but people in the industry who had come along to either support him or scorn him or to find out what the score was. Some of them had even brought their own booze.

"I'm sitting with Oldham and Malcolm Forrester at this boardroom table and people were cramming up against the table, pushing forward, they were virtually on top of us. It was more like a pop concert. It was unusual and totally different from any liquidation meeting I had been in, more like a social gathering than a formal thing. It was quite daunting and I had never handled anything like this. The creditors normally have a go at the directors for losing money but in his case, although there were creditors who had lost money it wasn't substantial. They all knew him. The only problem I had was trying to get order out of all these people because they were in the music business and to them it was a joke. I had great difficulty in reading out all the information about the company's history and they weren't really interested. They were talking amongst themselves, they were smoking; one or two were swigging from bottles. Normally the director has to answer specific questions raised from the floor, they get put through the mangle because the creditors want blood.

"The realisations of the company were put into a bank account, and the preferential creditors, the Inland Revenue, the Ratings Authorities — if rates were due, and employees for 16 weeks or more would get the first bite, then the second bite would be the liquidator for his fees and if there was anything left it would be distributed to the unsecured creditors *pro rata*. So if Oldham was owed £250,000 and the other creditors were owed £50,000, he would get five-sixths of what was left in the pot. But I don't think there was ever a distribution to unsecured creditors, Oldham didn't get anything back."

Steve Marriott told the *NME*: "Oldham was great about it. He just said, 'We're going under, mates'. He warned us all. He said, 'Get out now and sort yourselves out, get other labels because I don't want any of you going down with the company'. He was a great bloke, a right old blagger, but underneath the front he was a very nice man."

Jerry Shirley of Humble Pie: "Oldham did us the biggest favour that any single manager has ever done any band. As soon as he knew Immediate was going down he said, 'Call Jerry Moss at A&M'. We said, 'Okay'. Oldham said, 'You're not getting the point here, call Jerry Moss and he will sign you'. Oldham would have had the ability to hang us up in all kinds of legalities, which he chose not to do, he chose to give us a career that he felt we deserved. When Oldham said call Jerry Moss he also told us to ask for $400,000. We did and we got it."

Malcolm Forrester: "Dan Crewe was excellent at the creditors meeting. It was a funny meeting. Twinkle standing up while all these people are asking, 'Where are my royalties?' and 'Why haven't you paid the bills?' and then she says, 'Can I have my tapes back?'

"We closed Gloucester Place and I went to work at his house in Richmond. At that moment in time we still had Immediate Music, the publishing company. I was putting together this long list of songs Immediate Music owned; it was just incredible — a massive amount of songs we owned the copyright on. But the money wasn't there to pay United Artists. We owed them the remaining $175,000 on the $225,000 debenture deal. There was this clause in the deal, failure to pay meant forfeiting the entire Immediate Music publishing catalogue to United Artists. The money wasn't there. If it had have been there, it would have been paid. I don't think Andrew had that much money at that moment in time.

"This great catalogue of songs...' Forrester paused. Sighed. "Even then I'm sure I was thinking the amounts involved seemed small. I think United Artists made $175,000 from the Immediate catalogue within four months of taking it over. EMI own the catalogue now and over the years it's been worth millions and millions of pounds."

"I wasn't interested in Immediate in the last years at all," Oldham would reflect in a 1972 *Melody Maker* interview. "I started losing interest in the whole thing about six months after I parted company with the Rolling Stones. By that time Immediate had proved its point, so it became pretty boring. The last thing I was interested in was Humble

Pie. At the business end, the people there started believing the bullshit we were putting out about ourselves. In the last year, there was nobody really sitting there looking after the money. If the business had been run properly there was no reason why the company should have failed. But I don't feel bitter about that. I lost $250,000 personally. I'm the biggest creditor to the company. But it was worth it. Anything you learn out of is worth it. There was £85 left in the Immediate kitty after all the hassles. I really can't complain about it. Nobody really got burned, they can scream and holler all they want but nobody really got burned. That's the way God planned it."

THE END

Postscript

So what happened in the aftermath of the liquidation? Don Arden was given Oldham's gold eagle lectern but nothing else was salvaged from the Gloucester Place building — they couldn't even get the chandeliers down.

Together Oldham and Arden got up to a bit of naughtiness, earning a £10,000 advance from EMI on a single by a group that didn't exist. "And whattya call this group," Arden told me the EMI guy had said in the A&R meeting after listening to the fruits of a raucous recording session involving Oldham, Ron Wood and Peter Frampton. "Grunt Futtock," Oldham had growled. "Amazing," said the guy from EMI (as Don stifled a laugh). Then Oldham quit the UK for good to take up residence in the US, thus avoiding the huge tax bill that was pending.

He later told me: "The Rolling Stones and I were paying a third of everything we earned in the US straight as withholding tax, then when we'd bring back the 66.6% to England, they would want to tax us on the 100 per cent. Well, we didn't have it — it was gone. It had taken them three years to arrive at the figures so it had all been spent.

"If we'd had enough to settle the bill both the Rolling Stones and I would have had the option of staying in England but we didn't. The only way we had of getting out of paying the bill was this flaw in the law — if you left the country and didn't return for three years you were forgiven. That's what we all did; the Stones by mainly going to France and doing their *Exile On Main Street* album, me by going to Connecticut and New York."

The liquidation saw Immediate Records Ltd go under but the rights for the label outside of the UK remained

under the control of Immediate Records Inc, the US
company Oldham and Calder had set up in 1967 on the
back of the CBS deal. Oldham solely owned Immediate Inc
(having bought out Calder) and, once the deal with CBS[112]
for US rights wound down in 1970 he was free to assign
rights for the catalogue (outside the UK) to new companies.

In a deal that ran until 1975 Immediate Inc licensed
the rights to Europe to EMI. The concept of reissuing,
particularly before the introduction of CD, was still at a
primitive stage but select albums from the Immediate
catalogue would still sell in reasonable amounts, particularly
hits compilations or work by artists who had gone on to
bigger things.

In 1972 in the US Immediate Inc licensed the two
Humble Pie albums — Marriott's band having by then
made huge inroads in the US[113] — to Pie's then label A&M.
In 1975 the catalogue was licensed to Seymour Stein's new
indie label Sire for the US. That deal was all over the trade
press, with Immediate credited as "one of England's first
independent companies to succeed in the progressive field,
paving the way for today's giant British indies like Island,
Chrysalis, Charisma and Virgin".

"A great part of my life and energies are tied closely

---

112. The $7 million court case Oldham brought against CBS having
fizzled out.

113. After signing to A&M, Dee Anthony took over as manager and
focused on the US market. The band discarded the acoustic part
of their set and instigated a more raucous sound with Marriott as
front man. Despite the failure of their next album, *Humble Pie*, the
band quickly became known for popular live rock shows and in
July 1971 opened for Grand Funk Railroad at their historic Shea
Stadium concert, an event that broke the Beatles record for fastest-
selling stadium concert to that date. Clem Clempson replaced Peter
Frampton in 1972 and their next album, *Smokin'*, reached no.6 in the
US. Two more albums and a farewell tour followed before the group
disbanded in 1975.

to Immediate," Oldham told the press at the time, adding, "Sire[114] is probably the one company that I could entrust with the repackaging and marketing of Immediate. They were there on the scene during the Immediate years and have a first-hand knowledge of this all-important period in pop music. With their other repackages, they have proven that they have the necessary historical consciousness to produce a tasteful and authoritative package that will appeal to collectors."

In this period Oldham told me advances from US deals and royalties from EMI earned him approximately $250,000. Oldham was owed the payback — and this he took. And if Oldham had not taken the $250,000, he said "it would have gone to the Liquidator, Patrick Meehan Jnr or Tony Calder".

Calder was back on the scene with a new business partner, Patrick Meehan Jnr (whose dad was Don's one-time enforcer Patrick Meehan Snr) and in 1976 they bought Immediate Records Ltd from the liquidator for around £20,000. They had big plans for the back catalogue centred around a Small Faces reformation.

Oldham, meanwhile, travelled to Paris in 1975 and signed a new deal via his Immediate Inc for licensing on the Immediate back catalogue in Europe with Charly Records owned by Jean Luc Young who was on a buying spree, having just completed the purchase of the back-product from the Sun, Red Bird and Blue Cat record labels. His capture of Immediate made the front cover of UK trade magazine, *Music Week*. Oldham said he was more than happy to do the deal. "Jean Luc was independent, he cared

114. Founded in 1966 by Stein and Richard Gottehrer, Sire introduced underground British bands to the American market including the likes of Barclay James Harvest, Tomorrow, Matthews Southern Comfort and proto-punks The Deviants. The label made its name later by recording Talking Heads, The Undertones and, most famously, Madonna.

about things, and it was perfect for the kind of figures the Immediate stuff was going to do," Oldham told me. "It was a respectable home for that time."

Paul Mozian, an Allen Klein employee then working for Oldham, told me: "We called Jean Luc Young 'Kid Cash'. He was a young guy, like a scallywag, a street ruffian that had some money, we could never really figure out where his money came from. He wanted to establish a record label; he really had the hots for the Immediate thing. He was so delighted to be able to get the licensing for Europe.

"We did the deal in Paris and we were staying at the Paris Hilton. The management were not overwhelmed with Andrew. He had a tendency to insult other guests in the coffee shop. I would cringe. He wanted to be a tough guy so he would say stuff to people and 99 per cent of the time he would get away with it. This sort of thing escalated at the Paris Hilton to the point where they wanted us to leave and were threatening to call the police. Of course, they wanted him to sign the outstanding bill, which must have been $4,000 at this stage. There was much commotion in the lobby upon our departure as Andrew leapt on the front desk, threatening a hotelman that he insisted was a holdover from the Nazi occupation. Both our ladies were crying at this point and we made a hasty exit. Kid Cash came up with £10,000 and I was actually able to go to his bank account in Geneva and cash the cheque. Then Kid Cash brought the [Immediate] stuff to the UK and that's when the trouble began, between the Meehans, Charly and Andrew: we had to sort it out. I met Don Arden in England who was gonna help Andrew against Patrick and Tony. I guess Andrew figured Don Arden would be a good powerhouse at the time."

Oldham agreed to meet Calder and Meehan at the Midem Music Festival in Cannes for a discussion to clear the air on a yacht navigated by Don Arden who was now managing Black Sabbath. When I asked about the ensuing events, particularly about the claims of a gun being put in Calder's mouth, Arden joked: "What's the matter? Did someone forget to pull the trigger?"

Calder and Meehan made a good fist of re-launching Immediate in the UK. 'Itchycoo Park' made it back in the UK Top 10 and the Small Faces briefly flickered back to life. Marianne Faithful was on board and a series of Immediate compilations appeared on vinyl. This was still the pre-CD reissuing boom. Then Meehan dumped Calder and sold Immediate Records Ltd to Castle Music for a sizeable profit in 1983. Castle milked the catalogue for the next 17 years, mostly on CD. Castle largely restricted their Immediate operations to the UK, while Charly continued to exploit the Immediate back catalogue worldwide. Castle was acquired by Sanctuary Records, then the largest independent record company in the world, in the early 2000s. Sanctuary spent big on repackaging Immediate product and issued endless high-end CD box sets and compilation hits packages[115].

In 2002 Oldham appeared at London's High Court to launch a legal battle against both Sanctuary and Charly Records over their ownership of elements of the label's back catalogue: rights and royalties on master recordings he had paid for and leased to Immediate, and/or rights in acts (i.e. Small Faces, Amen Corner) that his money, not Immediate's, had paid for. He lost the case and the legal bills alone cost him £370,000.

Afterwards Oldham dictated to me a version of his side of the story and a description of the court case proceedings that was included in the 2008 edition of this book but cannot be printed here for legal reasons. The High Court case was widely reported in the media and much was made of 58-year-old Oldham's claim that many of the deals being debated in court had been made as a result of

115. Universal inherited Sanctuary's rights to Immediate when they took the company over in 2007.

his dependency on "drugs or drink", having been "out to lunch" for the years between 1967 and 1995.

I've come to know Rob Caiger a little since we first spoke in 1996; he managed the Immediate catalogue from Charly's London offices with style and commitment. It is a source of frustration for him that Oldham will not engage in any Immediate promotional activity. It's like having the crown jewels but no queen.

In late 2011 Rob and I were talking about doing something together for an Immediate box set special edition. There had been little news of fresh Immediate re-issues for many years. Caiger said that, in conjunction with Universal, he had spent over five years "protecting the catalogue, recovering lost tapes, and restoring and remastering material". He also said a lot of work had been done toward recovering and paying royalties and providing new, and fairer, contracts.

Caiger felt Oldham had been disrespectful toward Jean Luc Young in my original version of this book. He said that the proceedings in the 2002 court case were a matter of public record and that I had not accurately reflected the real reasons why the final judgement was made. Caiger said he was working happily with the surviving members of the Small Faces, Kenney Jones and Ian McLagan, on a remastered series of the band's work.

In April 2012 Small Faces were inducted into the Rock and Roll Hall of Fame. The same month Charly (in conjunction with Universal Music) rolled out remastered editions of the band's classic Immediate recordings with *Ogdens' Nut Gone Flake* as a centre piece. "This is the Small Faces as they should be heard," said Kenney Jones.

Loog Oldham was also inducted, alongside Brian Epstein posthumously, into the Rock and Roll Hall of Fame, in the 'Ahmet Ertegun Category' in 2014 but he refused to attend the ceremony, offended by the person chosen to induct him, some cat called Peter Asher[116].

On the Rock and Roll Hall of Fame website they write: "It's not an overstatement to say that Andrew Loog Oldham held the future of rock in his hands. He did PR for The Beatles, managed the Rolling Stones and produced such hits as 'Paint It Black', 'Get Off My Cloud' and 'I Can't Get No Satisfaction' — need we say more?" They did: "In 1965, Tom Wolfe famously dubbed Phil Spector "America's first tycoon of teen". Great Britain in the 1960s had its own version with Andrew Loog Oldham. Similarly eccentric, Oldham sported a one-of-a-kind mix of flamboyance, fashion, attitude, chutzpah, vision and business smarts. As co-manager of the Rolling Stones from May 1963 to September 1967, and founder and co-owner of Immediate Records from 1965 to 1970, he helped shape the future of rock, and turned the music industry in the United Kingdom on its head."

Caiger later helped me put together a CD of Steve Marriott music across the ages to accompany a *Mojo* feature promoting my authorized 2020 Marriott biography.

---

116. Peter Asher, CBE (1944-) is an English guitarist, singer, manager and record producer who came to prominence in the 1960s as a member of the pop duo Peter and Gordon before going on to a successful career as a manager helping to foster the recording careers of James Taylor and Linda Ronstadt among others. His sister Jane is Paul McCartney's former fiancée.

Afterword

Oldham is well and living in Colombia with his wife Esther. We have met occasionally since the court case and email regularly. I'm now older than Oldham was when we first met. Following the publication of *Stoned/2Stoned* Oldham rehabilitated his reputation and grabbed the modern, enjoying a respectable and healthy sunset to his career. He wrote more books, hosted a popular daily radio show on Sirius XM, lectured at universities [teaching 'Rock Dreams 1954-1984' during a 2020/21 tenure at Thompson Rivers University in Kamloops, B.C.], created his own podcasts and made acquaintances with a new coterie of acolytes such as Johnny Marr, and, of course, he went on to produce more music, often in Argentina with Charlie Garcia or the Ratones and their solo projects, but also in Canada.

In 2014 he recorded, with various guest vocalists complimenting the instrumentals, a sumptuously orchestrated and played album of Stones covers' *Andrew Oldham Orchestra and Friends play the Rolling Stones Songbook Vol. 2*. Included on the album was a version of 'Bitter Sweet Symphony' by The Verve. The moody 1997 football anthem was based around a repeated string riff from the Andrew Loog Oldham Orchestra's 1965 version of the Stones' 'The Last Time'. The Verve had been famously and unceremoniously steamrollered by Allen Klein soon after the song was a hit.

We talk about health and he is vastly knowledgeable on the subject, remains a great sounding board for life. He is light of heart, fast to humour.

I've known him so long. Said his name so many times.

Used him right up like he used me right up. I've done him no wrong. Kept everything tight. He let me put people on him: The Super Furry Animals were one (he hosted them in Bogota for a video shoot in the late 90s and singer Gruff sang on *Andrew Oldham Orchestra and Friends play the Rolling Stones Songbook Vol. 2.*) and now I can even tease him a little bit.[117]

And I've tried.

Mojo magazine asked me to get him to contribute to a feature on PP Arnold to coincide with her autobiography. He wouldn't. I suggested recently I publish the long list of records he has produced since 1963; several hundred, 60 years of music. In my opinion, there is no other British record producer who can hold a candle to him. It has always been a bugbear for me that this aspect of his career is often overlooked in favour of his reputation as starmaker and Svengali. Go ahead, he said, but he wasn't too fussed, certainly not interested in looking back and commenting.

We talked most recently about me publishing the full interviews of a selection of the people I interviewed for *Stoned* as a limited edition book and perhaps editing the many thousands of emails we exchanged 1997-99 for another fatter book (I'd found a two-foot pile of print outs going through my archive). He was on fire in that period I told him. Funny, warm, youthful, hot-wired yet

---

117. The Verve had obtained the rights to use the sample from the copyright holder, Decca Records, but just as the single was about to be released Klein, then head of ABKCO Records, refused clearance saying The Verve had used a larger portion than agreed. According to guitarist Nick McCabe, the dispute actually depended not on the sample but Ashcroft's vocal melody, which a musicologist determined was a half-time version of the Rolling Stones' 'Last Time' melody. Following a lawsuit, the Verve relinquished all royalties and Jagger and Richards were added to the songwriting credits. In 2019, following Klein's death, Jagger, Richards, and Klein's son ceded the rights to Verve songwriter Richard Ashcroft.

caring, precise, reflective, inquisitive and also demanding, admonishing, thorough and impish with his opinions. Real life was captured there.

"My seeds are already in your garden," he wrote back, "all you gotta do is dig."

backstage books

SIMON SPENCE is a renowned former writer for *i-D*, *The Face* and *NME* and collaborator on Andrew Loog Oldham's autobiographies *Stoned* and *2 Stoned*. He is the author of many acclaimed books on music including *The Stone Roses: War and Peace*, the authorised biography of Steve Marriot and *Still Breathing: The True Adventures of the Donnelly Brothers*.

ANTHONY DONNELLY is the entrepreneur behind the Gio-Goi fashion label that became synonymous with Madchester before becoming a worldwide brand. His headline-grabbing career has courted headlines and he has always had an interest in publishing, "from waiting outside newsagents to read my name in a paper at 5am to three decades' worth of marketing on the internet, I feel I know enough about publishing now to do this in a bigger and more experienced way. God help us all, the lunatics have finally built their own asylum!"

ASHLEY SHAW has been publishing books for 25 years. He is dedicated to giving people a platform to tell their story, even if they have never written a book before. A prime example of this is Karen Woods, who left school without being able to read or write but wrote 20 novels for Empire Publications before moving on to Harper Collins. Backstage Books represents an opportunity to widen this approach to publishing and bring new stories and new voices to a wider public.